A
GRAVEYARD
PRESERVATION
PRIMER

ABOUT THE SERIES
The American Association for State and Local History Book Series publishes technical and professional information for those who practice and support history, and addresses issues critical to the field of state and local history. To submit a proposal or manuscript to the series, please request proposal guidelines from AASLH headquarters: AASLH Book Series, 1717 Church St., Nashville, Tennessee 37203. Telephone: (615) 320-3203. Fax: (615) 327-9013. Web site: www.aaslh.org.

ABOUT THE ORGANIZATION
The American Association for State and Local History (AASLH) is a nonprofit educational organization dedicated to advancing knowledge, understanding, and appreciation of local history in the United States and Canada. In addition to sponsorship of this book series, the Association publishes the periodical *History News*, a newsletter, technical leaflets and reports, and other materials; confers prizes and awards in recognition of outstanding achievement in the field; and supports a broad education program and other activities designed to help members work more effectively. To join the organization, contact: Membership Director, AASLH, 1717 Church St., Nashville, Tennessee 37203.

A
GRAVEYARD
PRESERVATION
PRIMER

LYNETTE STRANGSTAD

ALTAMIRA
PRESS

A Division of
ROWMAN & LITTLEFIELD PUBLISHERS, INC.
Walnut Creek • Lanham • New York • Oxford

Published in cooperation with the Association for Gravestone Studies

ALTAMIRA PRESS
A division of Rowman & Littlefield Publishers, Inc.
1630 North Main Street, #367
Walnut Creek, CA 94596
www.altamirapress.com

Rowman & Littlefield Publishers, Inc.
A wholly owned subsidiary of The Rowman & Littlefield Publishing Group, Inc.
4501 Forbes Boulevard, Suite 200
Lanham, MD 20706

PO Box 317
Oxford
OX2 9RU, UK

Design by Gillian Murrey

British Library Cataloguing in Publication Information Available

Library of Congress Cataloging-in-Publication Data

Strangstad, Lynette.
    A graveyard preservation primer / Lynette Strangstad.
        p. cm. — (American Association for State and Local History Book Series)
    Originally published: Nashville, TN: American Association for State and Local
    History in cooperation with the Association for Gravestone Studies, c1988
    (The AASLH primer series).
    Published in cooperation with the Association for Gravestone Studies
    Includes bibliographical references and index.
    ISBN 0-7619-9130-1 (pbk: alk. paper)
        1. Sepulchral monuments—Conservation and restoration—United States.
    2. Cemeteries—Conservation and restoration—United States. I. Association for Gravestone
    Studies. II. Title. III. Series
    NB1855.S77   1995
    736'.5'0288—dc20   95-45229
                                                                     CIP

Printed in the United States of America

CONTENTS

FIGURES

FOREWORD

For ten years the Association for Gravestone Studies has noted with a mixture of relief and concern the growth of public interest in America's historic graveyards. Today mail and telephone requests for information and assistance relating to graveyard preservation exceed the number of requests the Association receives on all other subjects combined.

Fortunately AGS is in close touch with leaders in the field of stone conservation. Unfortunately, on the other hand, stone conservation is a complex and fast developing field with much research in progress so that there are few simple, across-the-board answers to questions about preserving and restoring graveyards.

We at AGS felt an obligation to answer the groundswell of inquiries by offering a book that would describe recommended procedures, but in view of the state of the art, we were hesitant. While we hesitated, action was being taken, not all of it good. Gravestone restoration projects, some large and well funded, others involving a few unpaid volunteers, sprang up and proceeded without expert guidance on the theory that it is better to do something than nothing. As a result much time was wasted and money poorly spent. Worse, the overall life of many treated stones was diminished rather than lengthened. A distressing follow-up to the misguided projects has been the appearance of a spate of hastily prepared how-to publications, most of which advocate some questionable or inappropriate procedures. Dissemination to the public of this material enlarges and prolongs the problem.

The call was clear. We could not wait for research to give us better ways to preserve stone. We not only had to tell eager, would-be restorers what they must not do; we had to tell them what they can do and how to do it properly. We needed an author with enthusiasm tempered with prudence, a person with a sound philosophy of historic preservation and restoration and who had extensive hands-on experience restoring historic graveyards. We asked Lynette Strangstad, who is familiar with historic yards from Halifax

ix

to Savannah, to write a book on graveyard preservation. Her company, Stone Faces, in Charleston, South Carolina, offers services in stone conservation and specializes in graveyard preservation. We asked Carol Perkins to make drawings to illustrate the book. My wife and I contributed photographs from our collection. Finally, we were fortunate to be able to join forces with the American Association for State and Local History with its excellent reputation in the field of historic preservation and to benefit from its expertise in editing, publishing, and distributing the book.

From the beginning we sought the personal and professional opinions and advice of leaders in various aspects of gravestone and graveyard preservation and restoration, and we were consistently gratified by their helpful suggestions and their overall encouragement in the development of this work. Conservators to whom we owe special thanks are Lance Mayer of the Lyman Allyn Museum in New London, Connecticut; Frank Matero of the Center for Preservation Research at Columbia University; and William N. Hosley, Jr., curator and conservation manager of the cemetery restoration project in Hartford, Connecticut. Barre Granite Association of Barre, Vermont, made a generous gift to the Association of Gravestone Studies, which defrayed some of the prepublication costs of this book.

A Graveyard Preservation Primer has been three years in the making. On behalf of the Association for Graveyard Studies, I wish to thank for their patience the many interested and eager people who have been waiting for this help before proceeding with projects to preserve their historic yards. For myself and for the Association for Gravestone Studies, I would like to thank Lynette Strangstad, the author, with whom I worked closely in the preparation of the book. Her high standards, her attention to detail, her scholarly yet practical approach to the subject, and her pleasant and cooperative manner made this effort a pleasure and the final result a milestone in gravestone literature.

DANIEL FARBER, *President*
ASSOCIATION FOR GRAVESTONE STUDIES
APRIL 5, 1987
WORCESTER, MASSACHUSETTS

For further information about The Association for Gravestone Studies, please write The Association for Gravestone Studies, Executive Director, 30 Elm Street, Worcester, Massachusetts 01609.

PREFACE

The purpose of this book is to acquaint the reader with the various aspects of graveyard preservation. It is, in a sense, a how-to manual, although I make no pretense of giving complete and definitive coverage of any of the subjects explored. It is intended specifically for nonprofessionals involved in small to mid-sized projects who are having difficulty in getting started because of the lack of staff or resources that are readily available to those in larger cities or those who are managing larger projects. Still, preservation of early graveyards is largely an unexplored field, and it is believed and hoped that much of the information contained within these pages will be useful to anyone, professional and nonprofessional alike, interested in the preservation of an early graveyard.

To those who have picked up this book with the intention of quickly learning how to "restore a graveyard" by themselves, this word of caution: stone conservation is a technical field involving training and developed skills and requiring years of experience; likewise, the preservation of an entire graveyard is an involved process generally requiring careful planning and the efforts of many concerned individuals. Thus, I offer no easy solutions here. This book does, however, describe procedures and direct you to some of the resources available; it will therefore help you begin to sort out the process and to make good decisions. Both the ideal and the realistic situations are often suggested, leaving choices to be made according to what is possible within the limitations of a particular group.

Fortunately graveyards are finally beginning to be recognized for the important resource they are. This book emerged as a response to the question that is being asked with increasing frequency: "What can I do to preserve this graveyard?" After following the suggestions outlined here, you should be able to make a sensible evaluation of the situation and to proceed efficiently, avoiding the common mistakes and waste of resources that characterize many well-intended graveyard preservation projects.

Most of the research available regarding gravestones concerns the earliest

East Coast stones, and my comments regarding the history of early stones and the people who dealt with them reflect the existing research. Likewise, illustrations regarding stone conservation problems and techniques have come to me primarily through my own work, much of which has been done in and around Charleston, South Carolina. Thus, many of the photographs used in this book are from the earliest American eras of that area. I believe that the photographs used provide excellent examples and demonstrate as well as any the focus of this book. Except for problems that can be seen as idiosyncratic to a given locale or region, most of the major problems and stone types found in any graveyard are dealt with in the following pages. I leave to other researchers and photographers the chronicling of the many important stones and graveyards of other historical eras and geographical areas than those represented here.

No book, however small, is created without the efforts of many people. I would like to thank those who in one way or another assisted in the preparation of this book. Special thanks go to Jessie Lie Farber, who labored many hours in helping to hone many words into a workable tool; to Daniel Farber, for permission to use his fine photographs; to Carol Perkins, for creating many of the diagrams in the book, and to Diane Issa for creating others; and to the Association for Gravestone Studies and Francis Duval for allowing use of the latter's diagrams. AGS and the editor of *Markers*, Theodore Chase, and executive director Rosalee Oakley deserve thanks for their assistance and encouragement and for allowing adaptations of some of their own earlier publications. Thanks, too, to the readers, including Frances Gale, Henry Lie, Frank Matero, Lance Mayer, and Thomas McGrath, who offered their time and expertise in critiquing early drafts, to B. J. Berry for his continued assistance in site work as well as in draft preparations, and to numerous others who offered their time, bits of information, encouragement, and assorted assistance. To all these my sincere thanks.

LYNETTE STRANGSTAD

1

ASSESSING THE PROBLEM

The Importance of Early Graveyards

Perhaps the first question that must be asked is why bother to preserve graveyards at all? After all, a great deal of cost and effort is involved, and land today is a scarce resource. There have been demands to turn some graveyards over for other uses. Many consider graveyards, or at least an interest in preserving them, to be morbid. Perhaps graveyards, like so many other evidences of an earlier time, should be allowed to disintegrate and return to the dust to which all things must eventually succumb.

One who indulges in such a line of thought, however, should also consider the real value of these early stonecarvings, some of the earliest art and written history available in the United States today. These early stones are archaeological artifacts. Unlike most such artifacts, they are readily available and in the same location as they were originally placed. Clearly, much can be learned about our American forebears from studying the stones.

Selection of materials indicates what these early settlers found available and what importance they placed on remembering their deceased family members. In some cases, the local materials proved to be a lasting tribute; in others, they have weathered to obscurity. In affluent communities, and with the advance of culture in this new country, sophisticated Americans chose from Carrara marbles, English limestones, and New England slates, each of which had its own attraction and was either unavailable locally or available only in limited areas. Local materials were passed over in favor of the exotic, prestigious, and in some cases, longer-lasting materials from afar.

This early interest in superior materials can reveal to us the trade routes and commercial patterns that were established, sometimes at surprisingly early points in history. Tracing such early routes gives us an idea of where trading was common as well as the relatively early sophistication of trade, particularly in coastal areas. Farther west, the difficulty of transporting massive stone overland is evident for many years in the overwhelming use of local stone.

The quality of craftsmanship available to early colonists is evident in the execution of design and epitaphs. Even limited study of early stones reveals that simple artwork, that which is accurately called "folk art," exists often side by side with the sophisticated and complex carving of accomplished stone sculptors. Sometimes it is clear that local carvers influenced each other. Occasionally these individuals moved elsewhere within a circumscribed area; less frequently they moved to another area. Much can be learned about specific carvers and their histories by studying particular carving styles. Further interest leads to study of the designs themselves to learn something of the art and philosophy of the times.

Examination of early central motifs and border carvings suggests the development of symbols and an iconography, which changed both regionally and with the development of the country. From these carvings we learn of changing attitudes toward death and immortality at different periods in American history. Here we gain a glimpse of the values held by our forebears.

Central motifs carry dramatic depictions of death, such as skulls and crossbones, scythes, and hourglasses, all indicating mortality and one's time cut off. As time passed, and perhaps as life became less harsh in the colonies, cherubs or soul effigies, as they are known, appear, possibly indicating ameliorating conditions and a greater emphasis on a life in the hereafter. Later motifs trace the progress of culture, with interest in classical portrait busts and occasional apparently representational portraits, followed by the neoclassical urn and willow by the turn of the nineteenth century. (See figure 1.)

Border motifs might carry symbols such as ears of corn, for example, a symbol of harvest, of fruitfulness, and a suggestion that the deceased have been fruitful in their labors and have themselves been harvested, called home, by their maker. A pineapple may reveal both the importance of hospitality in that day and also the welcoming of the soul to its heavenly home. Motifs that are similar to those commonly found in England, Scotland, Germany, and other countries at the same time suggest the importance to some early colonists of their ties to their mother country. And motifs bearing elements of architectural and furniture styles suggest parallel interest and development in these areas.

In addition, epitaphs reveal important genealogical information, sometimes otherwise lost in haphazard or destroyed early records. They give important social and cultural information ranging from statistics that can be gathered regarding age and sex of those who were born or died in a particular year; to statistics regarding those whose stones indicate succumbing to early diseases and periods of plague; to less direct information such as attitudes toward women in a given community at a given time. These are suggested by the size of women's gravestones and the intricacy of their carving, as well as by titles of address and inscriptions indicating desired feminine attributes.

Some of the most personal history to be found regarding early inhabitants resides in graveyards. A single family plot may tell of the early demise of the young doctor who specialized in herbal cures. It may also reveal the death of his young wife upon giving birth to their third daughter, who lies buried with her. A second daughter, the same plot may tell, never married, while the first daughter married a merchant from England, and they and their family lie in the plot adjacent to the first. This plot and a second one adjacent to it may tell, too, that the only son married and had a son whom he named after his own father. Such intimate early histories of ordinary citizens are rare to find, except in graveyards.

Events of personal importance and historical interest are found in inscriptions as well, such as the survival of an Indian massacre by a New England woman, the drowning of two young men when one leapt into the river in an attempt to save his friend, or the wounding of a southern child who defended her younger brother from invading Tory troops. In addition, they record items of humor. Entire books have been written on the wry Yankee humor found on New England gravestones.

While it is the outstanding carving of an early stone or the gravemarker of a nationally recognized figure that receives most acclaim, the egalitarianism of graveyards should perhaps be most valued. Unlike most histories, graveyards record the lives of all, signify past existences, and recognize one commonality of us all. The history of rich and poor, famous and infamous alike, is recorded here. Histories of entire towns may be present only here, and elements of local history may survive here as nowhere else. Whether recording events of a colonial settlement in 1690 or a midwestern frontier town in 1860, graveyards are often the only record, the only artifacts remaining to tell of lives—of individuals and communities—struggled for, well-lived in the face of sometimes tremendous odds, and finally given up reluctantly or "with peaceful composure."

Individual graveyards may be of local, regional, or even national importance in recording the history of an area or that of its historic figures. It is

ere lyes Buried the

A.

In Memory

B.

Figure 1. Typical motifs on early gravestones. (A) Winged skull or "death's head."
(Desire Peronneau, 1740, Charleston, South Carolina.) (B) Cherub or "soul effigy."
(Charles Warham, 1779, Charleston, South Carolina.) (C) Portrait representing the
deceased. (Mary Owen, 1749, Charleston, South Carolina.) (D) A fine border design
of flowers and ears of corn (John Stanyarne, 1749, Charleston, South Carolina.) (E)
Urn and willow designs. (Mary Taylor, 1810, Sudbury, Massachusetts.) All photo-
graphs by Daniel Farber.

not uncommon to hear of a quarter of a million dollars being invested in
the restoration of the house of a prestigious historical figure. Yet such a sum
to preserve the graveyard that could relate the history of an entire city is rare.

In addition to these historic functions, early graveyards, particularly in urban
settings, serve as park areas and green spaces, pleasant and needed areas of
respite from the concrete intensity that makes up so much of most urban
environments.

Early graveyards are outdoor museums, containing some of America's earliest examples of the stonecarver's art, an all but lost traditional art form. Each tombstone is an irreplaceable historical document, containing some of America's earliest written history. The ready accessibility of these museums allows all of us, not only historians, to view, to appreciate, to study these documents, to enjoy their artwork, to learn of our own history. They are invaluable educational tools through which we can teach our history to new generations, through which we can impart a sense of our historic past.

A civilized society values its past, its history, and it values its natural environment as well. If we are that society, we have a strong investment in our early graveyards and must work to protect that investment.

A Few Definitions

Popular usage gives considerable latitude to the many terms concerned with graveyard improvement. Within this publication, the following definitions apply.

Preservation. The act of protecting, maintaining, and saving. As commonly used, *preservation* has a broad meaning that includes both conservation and restoration. In the context of *graveyard preservation,* the term includes the care of graveyards and documents as well as the procedures applied to the stones themselves.

Conservation. Though the layman tends to use the words *conservation* and *preservation* interchangeably, the term *conservation* defines a specialized field involved with the stabilization, protection from deterioration, and preservation from loss of objects of historic and artistic value. *Gravestone conservation* concerns the skilled technical procedures used to repair and stabilize gravestones and monuments.

Restoration. The act of restoring—that is, of reconstructing, repairing, renewing. As commonly used *graveyard restoration* includes both preservation and conservation; in the context of this book, however, the distinctions noted above will generally be maintained.

Cemetery. A place set apart for burying the dead. The word, which derives from the Greek word for sleeping chamber, became popular in the nineteenth century.

Graveyard. An early cemetery. *Graveyard* is the term most often used here rather than *cemetery,* since this book focuses primarily on early burying grounds. The distinction is used here to differentiate historic burial grounds of the seventeenth, eighteenth, and nineteenth centuries from modern cemeteries.

Developing a Plan

Before making any changes to an old graveyard, take the time to determine what preservation work is needed and how it can best be done. Establish priorities. What are top priorities for a particular yard, and what can be relegated to a less-urgent status, perhaps even a second phase of the project? Prepare a comprehensive plan that is carefully thought out, organized, and practical. Good initial planning will save time and effort later on.

This planning need not be delegated to professionals, for in most cases the initial plan can be developed most effectively by those who are most involved, the people intimately concerned about the welfare of the old yard.

Consider the following eight points and decide how to approach each. Identify and begin work on projects that can be handled by untrained, unpaid volunteers, but simultaneously begin raising funds for the work that will require professional expertise.

In assessing the situation and making plans, these are among the questions to ask:

1. What legal body has jurisdiction over the graveyard? Is it municipally owned, church owned, or privately held land? What are the local ordinances governing cemeteries in the community? What are the pertinent laws of the state? Can you get permission to carry on conservation-related activities in this graveyard? It is essential that you be familiar with the applicable cemetery regulations, if any, before beginning any phase of a preservation project. Get permission and advise authorities of the scope and intention of your proposed work. In some cases a permit or other authorization must be obtained to keep the project within the bounds of the law.

2. What is the present level of security in the graveyard? Does the graveyard need additional security? If so, does that mean a fence, a wall, lighting, police surveillance, closing the graveyard at dusk? Are there other options? What will be most effective? What can you afford? What responsibilities can you assume? Try to pinpoint the individuals or organizations whose advice and services should be solicited.

3. Does documentation of the markers and their inscriptions exist? If so, when was it done, and is this documentation available? Does it need upgrading, revising? If so, who is best qualified to accomplish the task? What should a good document include? How much of the work can be done by volunteer help?

4. What restoration or conservation work is required? Who can best do it? How will you find that person or firm? How will you know when you

have found the right professional help? How much will it cost? Can you realisti-
cally expect to raise this amount? If you cannot secure funds for a complete
restoration, which stones should you choose to have repaired? What criteria
will you use for your selection? How much of the work, if any, can be done
with unpaid volunteer workers?

5. Should you make an archaeological survey? Why? What does an archaeological survey entail? What does it accomplish? What does it cost? Who could
do it?

6. What is required in the way of landscaping? Is a landscape architect
necessary? Who will do the work? What will it cost? How will the grounds
be used and maintained?

7. How can you promote and maintain public interest in the preservation
of the graveyard? Would it be useful to develop a walking tour or a brochure
to guide visitors to the most significant historical and artistic markers? What
educational, civic, or social organizations might have an interest in such a
tour or brochure and offer their support? Are there members of your group
who could organize a tour or prepare a brochure? What media coverage of
your project might be appropriate? What other publicity would be useful?

8. How do you go about securing funds for a project such as you are planning? Does your group have access to the services of a local fund raiser who
might give you tips on where to begin, even if you cannot afford to pay for
professional fund-raising services initially? What potential sources of funds
exist for your project? For example, are any descendants of people buried
in the graveyard still living in the area? Might they be interested in helping
to upgrade and maintain the burial site of their ancestors? Are there any
government grants or privately funded grants that might be applicable? How
do you find out? Do you know any grant writers? What information do you
need before preparing a grant proposal? Are some aspects of the project easier to find funding for than others? Can you tailor your grant applications
to those specific aspects? Can you begin work for which you have funding,
even if funds for the overall project are slow in coming? Would a fund-raising
brochure be useful? Who could prepare it?

Many of these questions will be dealt with on the following pages, but
none can be treated thoroughly enough to eliminate the need for your own
thoughtful investigation of each concern. Moreover, your situation will present unique problems as well as solutions with which only you can deal.

If a careful assessment and a comprehensive plan may seem a belabored
approach, you should be aware that no funding organization is going to pay

any attention to you unless you can first demonstrate a clear need and the ability to satisfy that need. Moreover, the early clarification of your goals and of the responsibilities of each member of your team within the framework of those goals will help the entire project proceed smoothly.

2
ORGANIZATIONAL CONCERNS

Gravestone Rubbing

On a sunny day in a popular graveyard, one may see schoolchildren rubbing stone images for a class, novice rubbers entertaining themselves with the newfound pleasure of creating images of angels and skulls, and serious stone rubbers who have elevated the activity to an art form. In many cases individuals "discover" early graveyards through this interest.

Creating a gravestone image on paper by rubbing chalk, crayon, or other media on a piece of paper placed over the gravestone is a popular graveyard activity. A good image is obtained fairly easily, and interesting effects can be created as well. A record of a full-sized individual stone that duplicates all the defects of the stone as well as the inscription can be made fairly quickly. Many people who are interested in old graveyards have either enjoyed the stone rubbings of others or have undertaken gravestone rubbings themselves.

Still, the subject of gravestone rubbing can be controversial for those involved with the preservation of a graveyard. Much permanent damage is done each year to the many early graveyards regularly visited by rubbers. Since most rubbers who have damaged stones would almost surely admit to some degree of fondness for the stones if asked, we must assume that damage occurs primarily for one of the following reasons:

1. Individuals unfamiliar with early gravestones assume that the stones are impervious to damage or that even if damage should occur, it is not of importance or can be easily reversed.

2. Individuals feel that they know the proper procedure to use in making stone rubbings; in fact, however, they do not (figure 2).

3. Children are left unsupervised, or virtually so, while parents carefully

Figure 2. This fine slate stone has been defaced by a careless rubber. (Jane Cazneau, 1784, Boston, Massachusetts.) Photograph by Daniel Farber.

prepare their own rubbings in another corner of the graveyard. School groups may also come to make rubbings without the benefit of adequate supervision. In their enthusiasm, children may forget the cautionary instructions given earlier.

To avoid such potential damage overseers of many early graveyards are choosing to limit gravestone rubbing activities or to prohibit them altogether. Controlling activities in a graveyard is nearly always of benefit, but curtailing them altogether sometimes has negative results. As in any circumstance where individuals are prohibited from activities of their interest, a few will violate such prohibitions with impunity, and others will harbor anger toward those who would impose such regulations, holding such limitations to be a curtailment of their rights.

Since one of the goals of most graveyard groups is better community support and public education, in some cases outright banning of gravestone rubbing is ill-advised. Nevertheless, for graveyard projects that do not desire to prohibit rubbings altogether, regulations for those who would enjoy the privilege of rubbing these early artifacts are highly appropriate.

Some cemetery managements require visitors to register with a two-part form: the first part remains with the cemetery and contains the rubber's name, address, and group association if any, along with a signed statement acknowledging responsibility for any damage done while rubbing. The second part, which stays with the rubber, grants permission to rub in that graveyard on that day and contains the regulations regarding stone rubbing in that yard. Any official of the graveyard will thus know at any time who is authorized to work in the yard and who is not, simply by requesting to see the permission form.

Some yards also require a small admission fee for the privilege of using the yard. In many graveyards it would be cumbersome or impossible to enforce a rubbing-fee regulation, but in some popular urban graveyards and cemeteries a sign instructing rubbers to sign in and pay at the parsonage or caretaker's quarters or town hall discourages careless rubbing practices. The money collected usually goes toward the maintenance of the yard.

Most people who are seriously interested in stone rubbing are more than willing to pay a small fee for the care of the yard. Those who are not much interested in the yard may be less inclined to pay the fee, and thus, some potentially careless individuals may be discouraged from using the yard. The regulation can be a relief to the careful, respectful rubber, and is preferable to banning rubbing altogether.

In Europe many of the most important brasses have, in fact, been replicated in recent years, and a fee is charged for rubbing not the precious original but a replica cast from the original and placed in the church for this purpose. To date, I know of no American graveyard that provides rubbers with a replica of its finest, most frequently rubbed stone, but the European practice bears consideration.

A set of regulations, as the following, with the addition of any special ones that apply to a particular yard, will outline what behavior is acceptable in the graveyard.

Regulations for visitors

1. The graveyard is open from 12 noon until dusk weekdays, and from 8 a.m. until dusk on weekends [or appropriate hours for a particular yard].

2. The graveyard management is not responsible for injury to visitors.

3. No running or jumping on stones or swinging or leaping from stone to stone is permitted. Failure to comply could result in serious damage to both visitors and stones.

4. Children in the graveyard are to be supervised at all times. Children under ten years of age shall not rub stones even with supervision.

5. Limit gravestone rubbing to sound stones only. Before proceeding, check each stone for stability. If a given stone appears fragile or unsound in any way, *choose another stone.*

6. Limit the cleaning of a stone to dusting with a soft-bristled brush. Do not attempt to remove lichens or moss that may be growing on stones. Never use a wire brush on gravestones.

7. Use a heavy grade paper so wax or ink does not bleed through onto the stone.

8. Cover the image amply with paper to avoid overrubbing onto the stone. *Do not make any marks on the stone.*

9. Attach paper with masking tape to the *back* of the stone. Be sure to remove all bits of tape from the stone and nearby ground before leaving.

10. Avoid rubbing deeply carved stones. Such stones can be easily damaged and generally do not make good rubbings anyway.

11. Avoid rubbing marble or other stones with coarse-grained textures, as coloring agents may bleed through the paper onto the stones.

12. The best choice of stones for rubbing are slate stones in good condition with low-relief or incised carvings. These produce the best images on paper and are less easily damaged inadvertently.

13. Check the work site before leaving to be sure no tape, paper, or trash has been left behind.

See appendix A for a sample registration form with regulations for gravestone rubbing.

Working with Volunteers

Volunteers will be a large part of the work force of many small to midsized projects. They may help to establish priorities, create plans, solicit funds, and provide much of the other labor that will be required. The involvement of a large number of volunteers in a complex project requires not only careful planning but also a volunteer coordinator. This individual bears the responsibility for setting up timetables, working within the timeframes of the volunteers, assigning tasks to appropriate volunteers, and following up to see that each task is completed in timely fashion so as not to delay subsequent steps in the process. In large part, the volunteer coordinator tries to maintain harmony by ensuring that each member of the group understands the goals and priorities of the project and his or her role within the overall effort. When professionals are involved, whether in consulting roles or actual restoration efforts, the coordinator takes care of the nuts-and-bolts items, usually by delegating tasks, such as making telephone calls, providing lunch for the all-day training seminar held on the grounds, and arranging for news coverage by preparing press releases or by informing reporters and photographers of publicity events. Ideally, the person in this position is paid rather than being a volunteer; when that is not possible, a dedicated individual with much time and good organizational skills must be found for the project to proceed smoothly. Although some projects may succeed even in the absence of such a position, it should not be considered optional even for a mid-sized project.

Training workshops are essential for volunteers who are to become involved with actual hands-on preservation work. While trained volunteers are invaluable to the success of a graveyard preservation project, untrained and inexperienced ones can cause permanent damage. I strongly advise that, even when the procedures outlined here are followed, an on-site training program led by a graveyard preservation professional be a prerequisite to actual work. Volunteers can thus learn techniques by demonstration at a given site, where details idiosyncratic to the site are considered. Such a workshop is beneficial not only to those volunteers and staff interested in carrying out the work but also to others who may wish to use such skills at other sites. Training workshops prove to be a powerful public educational tool and an effective way to get the most out of graveyard preservation volunteer efforts.

Public Awareness

Whether you see it as a primary goal of your graveyard preservation project or not, public awareness will play a part in the way the project develops. Increased public awareness of the importance of an old graveyard is both a tool for and a product of your efforts. Educating the public to the histori-

cal, cultural, social, and artistic merits of graveyards benefits both your graveyard and others. Ways to increase public awareness are many and varied,
ranging from the very simple and informal to the professional and
sophisticated.

In the first place, it is exciting to share one's interests with others, and
in this field there are many who are eager to learn. Passing on bits of information in an informal way to graveyard visitors is usually rewarding for both
parties. Slide lectures given to schools and civic groups can stimulate students, teachers, and parents and can lead to a variety of additional projects.
Tours guided by knowledgeable members of the community can generate
excellent publicity. A printed guide or brochure featuring stones chosen for
their artistic, historical, architectural, humorous, or other features can serve
as an educational tool and as a fund raiser as well. Such publicatons, widely
distributed through libraries, churches, historical societies, and schools, promote interest that can pay off in both planned and unexpected ways. Some
groups sell graveyard guides to cover the cost of printing, while others sell
them at a profit, using the earnings to help defray the cost of graveyard maintenance. Guides also offer an opportunity to list closing hours and other pertinent information, such as regulations regarding stone rubbing or general
conduct in the graveyard.

Efforts of this kind generally reap double rewards. The first is the intended
one. The second is that of gaining community goodwill and potential allies
in protecting the graveyard. Schoolchildren who have come to know the old
yard and who have favorite stones there are less likely to become teenagers
who vandalize them or who stand mute while their peers do so. Adults who
appreciate the historical and artistic significance of the graveyard are more
likely to support a community preservation and maintenance program. Those
who understand and value the site are more likely to visit the yard; and increasing the pedestrian traffic is generally essential to reducing the time spent
there by the less constructive elements of the population.

Another method of increasing public awareness and respect is through good
signs. They will vary from one yard to the next and might include any of
the following:

Opening and closing hours. No trespassing after closing hours (posted signs
are often a necessary condition for effective police control).

Gravestone rubbing regulations.

Warnings of potential danger to visitors and to gravemarkers if the markers are used for climbing, jumping, swinging, and in some instances, for
just sitting or leaning. Even using a stone to pull oneself up from a seated

Figure 3. An example of an attractive sign that provides important information. Photograph by the author.

position can dislodge or snap a weak stone, causing a serious accident.

Appropriate educational and interpretive information, such as a brief history of the graveyard or map identifying significant stones (markers for important persons, stones signed by their carvers, stones with unusual motifs or epitaphs, etc.).

Information about an ongoing preservation project, listing major contributors and giving an address for donations.

The number to telephone to make inquiries and report problems. (See figure 3.)

Security

Because security is a concern about which people have strong feelings, deciding how to provide it usually generates considerable discussion. The discussion is, after all, the consideration of two opposites: the advantages of keeping people out of the old graveyard as opposed to the merits of encouraging the public to spend more time there.

The first step is to determine the current level of security and how it can be increased, if necessary. Problems with regulating visitors or with vandalism clearly indicate a need for additional security. If there are no such problems, perhaps even if the yard is not fenced or otherwise contained, the situation is better left alone. Sometimes changes precipitate problems that would not otherwise occur.

If improved security is necessary, consider these points. The function of a wall is to keep people out. But remember that solid walls also provide privacy to those within. Nearly anyone with the will can scale a wall, and once inside, intruders tend to go unnoticed, free to do as they please. An ironwork or rail fence may be easier to scale than a wall, but by providing visibility, it discourages vandalism and promotes the safety of the authorized visitor.

While urban open spaces are generally considered best protected at night with locked fences and good lighting, to lock graveyard gates by day discourages healthy pedestrian traffic and tends to create a refuge for derelicts and a meeting place for vandals.

Many graveyards, of course, are in remote, rural locations. In such cases local wisdom may best direct the course of action. Sometimes, for example, lighting such graveyards at night only provides better visibility to those who would steal from or cause damage to the yard.

Ask your local police how they would prefer to have you handle security. Establish a dialogue with them, for they can be among your strongest allies. Learn what they consider to be your part in maintaining the security of the graveyard, and hold up your end of the bargain.

Keep the graveyard well maintained. To do so creates a friendly, parklike atmosphere, encouraging the kind of traffic you want to promote.

Graveyards as an Educational Tool

Classrooms of schoolchildren sent to a graveyard to make rubbings of ancient stones open the possibility for considerable damage to occur; nevertheless, graveyards can be important educational tools within or outside of a school environment. Experience has shown that one of the best ways to protect graveyards is to educate the public that frequents them as to their importance and their charm. This applies to the general public, but particularly to schoolchildren, since introducing a new generation to the significance of gravestones goes far toward having a concerned adult populace in later years.

The creative teacher must operate fairly independently here, since not many lesson plans or suggestions for the use of graveyards in education programs exist. A few such resources are listed in the Sources of Additional Information at the back of the book.

Field trips make a graveyard "come alive" for children in the best sense of the phrase. Simply including early graveyards among the trips to museums and other cultural resources reinforces the fact that graveyards are among these treasures and are to be treated as the outdoor museums they are. Such trips are also effective in dispelling children's occasional fear of graveyards, which is often brought on by movies and shared stories.

Varying age groups will require different activities, of course. The few suggestions that follow are intended only to indicate the variety of activities and the various age groups that can be involved. A concerned teacher can develop programs that will fit the needs of a particular classroom.

A scavenger hunt to see who can find, for example, the most stones with cherubs on them; the most stones bearing dates before, say, 1776; the stone for the ninety-seven-year-old minister; the stone whose inscription indicates that the individual died of yellow fever or some other named misfortune.

An English lesson in which students seek out the nonstandard spellings of words common prior to about 1790, as well as archaic words or phrases, clear evidence of our changing language.

A history lesson in which students identify particular historical facts or personages on the stones themselves; or, for an older group, a research project to learn something of the personal history of an individual or family chosen from the yard.

An art lesson where students identify favorite stones; identify characteristics of the artwork common to many stones; identify characteristics that might suggest a particular carver; photograph stones; create original artwork using some of the same motifs or perhaps those more appropriate to a similar memorial if found today.

A *sociology lesson* in which students gather data for a particular decade, using the graveyard as the source. Different teams might gather information for different decades, and information for fifty years or a century might eventually be compiled, offering such information as number of births recorded in a given year or decade; number of deaths; median lifespan in a certain decade; number of deaths attributed to accident or disease; representation of a particular first name or surname in different decades; representation of various gravestone motifs in different decades.

A *geology lesson* in which students identify the variety of stones represented, examining typical characteristics of each type as well as unusual features in a given example.

A Word about Funding

Funding is rarely easy to obtain for any project, no matter how worthy. Funding for preserving an old graveyard may be particularly difficult to obtain, since the importance of preserving early graveyards is just beginning to be recognized. Don't postpone fund-raising efforts. Volunteers should be working on other early phases of the project while initial fund-raising activities are taking place. Plan to carry on an active fund-raising campaign simultaneously with all other early activities.

If the property is city or state owned, you may want to apply for an allotment for graveyard maintenance and repair in the next annual budget. If your organization has any experienced grant writers, set them to the task of seeking private foundation grants. A foundation headquartered in your locale may limit its funding to local projects and may be looking for a worthy project such as yours. Government grants are available occasionally, so keep in touch with your state historic preservation officer to get a lead on any applicable grants that become available.

Descendants of people buried in the graveyard are another possible funding source. Descendants can be hard to track down, but if found and properly approached, they can be very helpful. Sometimes they are looking for information regarding their ancestors, and they may be encouraged by current efforts, particularly if an offer to share any information regarding their family background is made, or if they are provided with copies of epitaphs, photographs of family tombstones or monuments, or other information about their family members.

Before seeking any grant support, document the most significant features of the graveyard, such as the gravesites of prominent individuals; any of the graveyard's firsts (earliest gravemarker, oldest burial ground in the city, state, county, province, etc.); and outstanding aspects of the yard to be preserved. Some research into the community's history, together with considerable on-site study of the yard and its makers, is very much in order. Seek the help of local scholars in the fields of art (especially folk art), American studies, geology, anthropology, archaeology, horticulture, genealogy, and religion. They may lead to a bonanza of information that will add strength to applications for funding. In addition, some of this information might further help the cause by appealing to a special interest or concern of the prospective funding organization. Funding may be more readily available for one aspect of the preservation project than another. All funding criteria for the agencies to be approached should be studied. A specific proposal to meet the special requirements of that agency can then be offered. Along with the disciplines listed above, consider also museum studies when applying for grants. A graveyard is, after all, an outdoor musuem. Also, before seeking grant support, document any work that has already been done, including work done with unpaid volunteer help. Sometimes such work is considered as in-kind donations when applying for matching funds.

Any National Landmark site related to the old yard (such as a church, meeting house, the home of one of the deceased buried in the yard, or a single famous gravesite) should be mentioned in grant applications. In fact, applying for National Landmark status may be in order. Although the designation as a National Landmark of a graveyard not contiguous with a related historic site is unusual, applying for landmark status has much in common with applying for funding for the preservation project—that is, the significance of the yard and the ability to put it into good condition and maintain it must be shown—so the two kinds of applications might work to the advantage of each other.

Conducting a local fund-raising campaign is usually essential, even when grant money is available. Granting agencies will want to know that available resources are being used before they commit themselves to involvement.

A local fund-raising campaign may include solicitation of the members of area historical societies and other organizations, such as the Daughters of the American Revolution, that are interested in the area's history. It may also include soliciting contributions from businesses and corporations that might benefit from the upgrading of a downtown area, for example, or from the good public relations involved. A garden club may choose to assist with landscaping. School and church groups may also be approached for help on the basis of the contributions the project may make to their particular interests and concerns.

A fund-raising brochure can be extremely useful in selling the project and publicizing the need for financial support. It should tell, in a nutshell, the significance of the graveyard, the scope of the proposed project, and its anticipated cost. Its appeal may be emotional, but its content should be factual.

Fund-raising efforts such as selling notecards, rubbings, guides, and the like should be considered, although the steady, relatively small income from sales of this kind may be best suited to helping provide increased public awareness in the area and continued maintenance after the project is completed. Another possible source of a small, steady income is a stone-rubbing fee.

3
COLLECTING DATA

Documenting the Yard

Documentation is an essential early step in graveyard preservation, providing a permanent record of an individual graveyard. In most cases, it can be done effectively by volunteers. Several elements are included in documenting a graveyard, and each is discussed below.

Existing Documents

The existence of early, and even of recent, documents can save much time in efforts applied to graveyard documentation. Check likely sources for existing maps and transcriptions of epitaphs that may have been made years ago and are all but forgotten. Places to start include church records, if the graveyard is or has been associated with a church; city records; local historical societies; local libraries; and individuals interested in and knowledgeable about activities concerning the graveyard. At some time a local group may have transcribed and photographed the entire yard, or at least parts of it.

Older photographs may reveal epitaphs no longer readable; they may indicate the condition of a particular stone ten, or even fifty, years ago; they may reveal the placement of stones no longer existing in the graveyard; and they may even suggest earlier layouts, landscaping, and the general appearance of the yard at some earlier point.

Existing transcriptions of epitaphs can save much time in providing written information regarding the graveyard. Such transcriptions, even if published, should be checked against the original stones when possible, in order to correct any earlier mistakes.

Existing maps, too, can be of much use, since they may need only minor updating. An early map may also tell of the location of stones now out of place and may suggest where stones presently missing are buried (if they broke and remained in their original locations, only to be gradually covered with sod).

Inscriptions

Inscriptions should be read directly from the markers. It is useful to work in pairs, with one person reading aloud and the other recording. The reader should take care to note the ending of one line and the beginning of another; capitalizations; nonstandard spellings; nonstandard lettering (use of the letter *J* for the numeral *1* or use the elongated *S*, for example; abbreviations, punctuation marks (and their absence); raised letters; words that are out of alignment or that even wrap around the margin of the letterings; and any other idiosyncrasies of the carver's lettering style. (See figure 4.)

Then send out a second team to transcribe the epitaphs again. Finally, have a third team compare transcriptions and check and correct discrepancies. Only in this way can you expect to get completely accurate transcriptions.

Lacking the manpower for such a thorough transcribing process, you could send out two teams or individuals to do a day's transcribing, then have the teams or individuals check each other's transcriptions the following day.

It is easiest to read the inscriptions when a strong sun strikes the carved face of the stone at a raking angle. A stone that is nearly illegible because its face is eroded, lichen-covered, or otherwise obscured may have to be checked many times under a variety of lighting conditions; the difference in the degree of clarity can be remarkable given different lighting (figure 5).

Mirrors

A mirror reflecting sunlight can be used to direct light at a raking angle onto the carved surface of a shaded marker (some markers are never fully lighted by the sun) or to gain greater clarity for reading or photographing a poorly lit stone. Moving the mirror to reflect the sunlight at a variety of raking angles will further facilitate the reading of a shaded, deteriorated inscription. If the shaded area around the marker is large, a partner can hold the mirror, reflecting the light from a sunlit spot some distance from the stone while the reader is positioned at the stone to decipher the inscription and transcribe. Bear in mind that the mirror only reflects existing sunlight and is of no use when the sky is overcast.

Rubbings are generally not of great help in the reading of deteriorated inscriptions, particularly if the marker has a grainy surface. Moreover, if the face of the stone is in poor condition, rubbing can further damage it. In

Figure 4. This inscription contains examples of eighteenth-century lettering peculiarities that should be accurately transcribed: for example, the long S in several words; abbreviations with raised letters (Efq ʳ); the line and commas under the raised th in dates (6ᵗʰ); the mix of uppercase and lowercase letters; and the placement of lines of inscription within the text. (Charles Otis, 1794, Charleston, South Carolina.) Photograph by Daniel Farber.

most cases, it is not advisable to attempt to clean a stone prior to reading it. Cleaning is a process that requires some familiarity with stones. If necessary, a dry soft-bristled brush or one dipped in plain water may be used. Sometimes clipping the grass growing in front of the stone will make reading easier. Further information on cleaning gravestones can be found in chapter 4. Mirrors are by far the superior tools to use in reading obscured inscriptions.

Figure 5. Document earlier repairs. These iron reinforcing bars have failed and may have damaged the stone. This is not a procedure now recommended, although it should be noted that such imperfect repairs may have saved some stones for today's restorers to mend. Photograph by Daniel Farber.

Recording Detailed Information about Each Gravemarker

A number of forms are available for recording pertinent data, although no form has been generally accepted as the best and standard form. A standard form would be useful to researchers in making compilations and comparisons involving many yards and would facilitate computer-generated comparisons and analyses of a particular yard. Whether you use one of the sample forms provided in appendix B or elect to fashion one of your own, the following data should be recorded:

Date of record
Name and location of the yard
Type of marker: headstone, footstone, crypt, vault, obelisk, etc.
Size of marker: above-ground height, width, thickness
Type and color of stone: such as pink granite, red slate, white marble, yellow sandstone, etc.
Identification number for each stone to correspond with map
Location of the marker within the graveyard
Condition of the stone: excellent, good, fair, poor. Specify problems, such as "missing right shoulder," "face spalling," etc.
Name of deceased and death date
Name of carver, if known
Ornamental carving: description and location on the stone of any generic motifs such as skull, winged angel, urn and willow, or other identifiable but less common motifs, such as corn, ivy, serpents, etc.
Other characterizing information.

See the Sources of Additional Information at the end of the book for publications dealing with gravestone symbols and decorative motifs, carver identification, and regional variations in carving styles. The Association for Gravestone Studies can provide more information.

Documentation of Repairs and Condition of Stone

Documentation should include all known repairs or preservation treatments that any of the stones has received in the past, plus, of course, those repairs and adaptations made in connection with the current preservation project. In addition, the present condition of the stone should be recorded (figure 6).

Diagnose the condition of each stone before proceeding with any work. Such a diagnosis is best made by an individual familiar with stone types and stone deterioration. In any case, indicate any previous repairs, presence of graffiti, biological growth, staining, efflorescence, erosion due to weather-

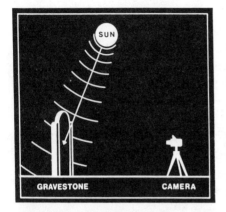
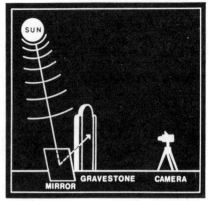
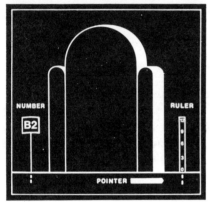

Figure 6. Techniques for reading and photographing gravestones. Strong sun at a raking angle is best for photographing gravestones (upper left); a mirror is used to reflect the sun's rays onto a shaded stone (upper right); these identifying items are used in photographic documentation (lower left).

ing, flaking, blistering, and exfoliation. Include, too, details regarding the context of the stone in the yard—whether or not it is tilted, is sunken, or has fallen over. Indicate stone losses, whether from details of the face of the stone, or larger losses, such as loss of a shoulder or a tympanum. Record fragmentation of stones, indicating how many pieces the stone is in, which pieces appear to be missing, where pieces are now located. All this information should be gathered before cleaning and resetting stones and even before cleaning up the yard (figure 7).

Carvers' Attributions

Determining the carver of a particular stone may not be an easy task, nor, in many cases, even a possible one. But many graveyards have a number of stones demonstrably by the same carver or perhaps from the same carving shop.

Attributions may be made most easily by a carver's signature found on the stone, usually on the bottom right-hand corner of the carved side of the stone. It may read "John Smith, carver" or "John Smith, sculptor" or "J.S., engraver." It may also indicate the city of residence of the carver, as "John Smith, Boston." Such an identification is fairly easy to make, although occasionally the signature may be on another part of the stone, such as the top or the edge or even in the tympanum. It often takes a careful eye to discover even a carved signature (figure 8).

A second method of determining attribution is through probate records of the deceased. Occasionally such records will indicate a sum of money paid to a carver for cutting a tombstone.

A third way of determining attribution is through identifying characteristics of the carving. This is the most uncertain method of carver identification. To an individual who is familiar with particular stones, however, common elements and common carving idiosyncrasies often become evident. Note the lettering, for example. Particular carvers may give peculiar flourishes to certain letters; they may capitalize words in an unusual but consistent manner; they may use the same border motif or footstone motif repeatedly; or there may be other identifying characteristics. Take care in making such identification, however, for many carvers worked together or copied features of an earlier or contemporary carver who was more skilled or more well known.

The carver's name, if discovered, should become a part of the documentation, along with a record of how it was determined. Later researchers can then confirm attribution or determine why a particular attribution was incorrect, even though it may have been made with the best information available at the time.

Photographs

Good black-and-white photographs are an essential part of the document. Although it is ideal to engage the services of a professional photographer to make this photographic record, a capable volunteer using a camera with a good lens can probably do the job. Artistic photographs are not required; what is needed are high-contrast photographs that clearly show the lettering, the decorative carving, and the stone's condition. Strong sunlight at a 20 to 30 degree angle to the stone can produce a high-contrast photograph.

In choosing a camera, consider negative size. A camera that produces a larger negative will produce a better enlargement; however, a camera that produces a smaller negative will probably be easier to handle and is less expen-

A.

Figure 7. Natural deterioration. (A) Erosion of marble. (Elanthan Hubbel, 1801, Bennington, Vermont.) (B) Exfoliation of sandstone. (C) Exfoliation of slate. (Martha Freeman, c. 1784, Storrs, Connecticut.) (D) Flaking of slate due to delaminating of fine layers of stone. (Joseph Thacher, 1763, Yarmouth, Massachusetts.) All photographs by Daniel Farber.

B.

C

D

A

B

sive to use. Many consider a 35mm camera excellent for photographing grave-stones, but other types of cameras also produce excellent records.

Informational guides, placed as a part of each photograph, can be very helpful in using it later. By properly placing a scale such as a ruler by each stone, the photographer can record the size of the stone. A pointer should be a part of each photograph in order to indicate orientation of the stone. If the pointer always points north, the viewer can readily determine which direction each stone is facing. An identification number alongside the stone will help to locate the stone within the graveyard or to identify it from among many transcriptions. Such informational guides should be freestanding along-side each stone; they should not be affixed to any stone. Lacking such guides, each photograph should be identified in a written log by size, identification number, and orientation. Log each stone as the picture is taken. (See figure 5.)

Occasionally a stone may be dusty or obscured by grasses. As noted earlier, cleaning stones should be avoided whenever possible. Some stones can be damaged by most cleaning agents. If necessary, a soft-bristled brush used dry or with water only will clean a stone well enough for photographing. For stones that are seriously marred by dirt and deposits and will be part of a later cleaning phase of the project, a "before" photo is extremely desira-ble. Grass that obscures a stone should be clipped before the photograph is taken.

The use of a mirror to light a shaded stone is as helpful in making a good photograph as it is in reading a shaded inscription. To light the complete stone this way, however, requires a mirror as tall as the stone. A lightweight door mirror often works well. In using a mirror to photograph stones, try to work with the sunlight behind the stone. Experiment to determine the best position of the mirror for a particular stone. In some cases a light strik-ing the stone from slightly above the stone will give the best image. If a stone is in shade, two mirrors may be needed to reflect the sun's rays to the desired angle. If the rays fall directly on the stone creating "flat" lighting, the stone may be blocked from the sun and shaded and a mirror used to direct rays for the desired lighting angle. (See figure 5.)

Figure 8. Carvers' signatures. Gravestone carvers sometimes sign their work, placing initials or full signatures in various locations on the stone. (A) Lemuel Savery signed this slate stone—"Lem ^{l} Savery fecit Pli^{mo} NE" (Lemuel Savery made it, Plymouth, New England)—under the epitaph. (Benjamin Hawes, 1781, Charleston, South Caro-lina.) (B) Henry Emmes placed his signature, "H. Emmes Boston," on the curved tympanum of this slate gravestone. (Elizabeth Simmons, 1740, Charleston, South Carolina.) Photographs by Daniel Farber.

An additional technique that facilitates photographing poorly lit stones is that of using a strobe light. Strobe light attachments are available for most single lens reflex cameras. Used with an extension wire, which allows the camera to be positioned in front of the stone, the strobe flash is positioned on a tripod at a raking angle to the stone for the necessary high-contrast shot. A little experience with the technique will eliminate irregularly lighted stones caused by improper placement of the light. This technique is further detailed in an article in the Spring 1987 issue of the "AGS Newsletter."

In addition to photographs of the whole stone, close-up photographs of details such as the tympanum carving or a signature are useful. If expense is a concern, reduce the number of prints made, filing just the negatives for the less important markers or for those of less immediate concern. This cost-saving method is preferable to reducing the number of stones photographed because the significance of a gravemarker is often not immediately apparent, and making a photographic record of a stone of considerable importance could easily be omitted. If more than one photograph is to be taken of each stone, many professionals recommend showing the stone in its surroundings, which may help further to identify the stone and its placement in future years. Then, for detail shots, a dark, solid-colored backdrop may be used, so that the surroundings don't detract from appreciation of artistic detail.

Mapping the Graveyard

An accurate map of the graveyard will have many uses while the preservation project is in progress as well as in the future. If an early map is available, check its accuracy. It may be useful in constructing the new map. It will surely show interesting alterations in the yard, and it may also be useful later in locating buried stones. Make no marks on the map; an early map is an important historical document in itself. If possible, have it reproduced and use the copies for updating.

If funding permits, and especially if the yard is large and complex, the ideal approach to map making is to provide an accurate survey by professional aerial photography or ground survey. Most often the map must be made by volunteers, however. The use of a grid system and the conscientious measuring of each stone from two fixed points will ensure a reasonably accurate map.

Prepare a base line, preferably following a boundary of the yard such as a wall or building. Select permanent landmarks such as corners of a building for the fixed points from which you will work, as later researchers may want to trace your steps in locating a stone. Clearly a tree that has since died or a stone that has since been removed will be of no use to them. If a fixed boundary is not available, construct a base line using a line and a 100-foot tape measure. Divide the base line into 10-foot sections using markers with flags. Then create accurate perpendicular lines in the field, measuring two points equidistant from one of the flag markers. Take two lines of equal length and bring them together in what appears to be a perpendicular fashion. The point where these lines actually meet is perpendicular to the base line. In this way 10-foot square blocks can be created in the field (figure 9).

On paper, plot the base line and the perimeter of the graveyard. Divide this into 10-foot-square sections to allow for ease in working. The work following will be easiest if the fixed points chosen for triangulation are also along the base line of the map. Establish and plot locations of major landmarks within the graveyard, such as a building, major monument, or large trees. Measure each stone from the chosen two fixed points, and plot each on the map. For greatest accuracy, determine the left edge of the stone from the fixed points and plot the right edge in the same manner.

A numerical system may be used to identify individual stones; the system may be further refined by identifying graveyard blocks by letter. The stones can then be located by block letter and individual number. In a large yard, proceed by mapping one block at a time, using the largest format that is comfortable to work with. Then coordinate all blocks to create a full graveyard overview. The individual block maps can be used for study or location of particular stones.

It is helpful to use a simple system of symbols to denote types of monuments and a numerical system to identify the stones (figure 10). The numerical system should be cross-referenced with an alphabetized list of the markers by name of deceased, so that stones can be located on the map and in the yard both numerically and alphabetically.

When the documentation of a graveyard is complete, file a copy in a permanent repository—the archives of a state or local historical society, the collection of a local museum or library, or some other safe and accessible storage facility. Ideally, several copies should be made and properly housed. One copy should be filed with the Association for Gravestone Studies, where it will become part of the association's permanent archives, accessible to researchers nationwide. In addition, a number of copies of at least the most frequently used data, such as the map, the transcription of epitaphs, and the list of names of deceased buried in the yard, should be kept locally with a caretaker or at a nearby church or other organization for use by interested

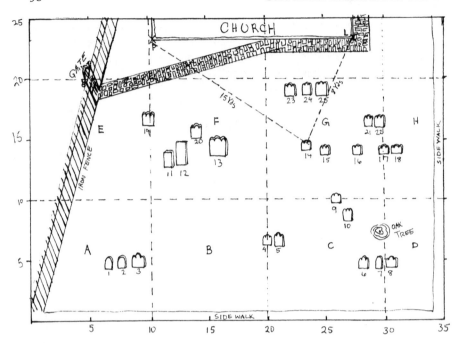

Figure 9. Mapping the graveyard by a grid system. Drawing by Diane Issa.

1. Look for any existing maps.

Check these for accuracy against existing conditions.

Save for reference later in locating buried stones.

Make no marks on old maps—these are historic documents.

If possible, make copies to use for updating.

2. Prepare a grid system for the yard you're mapping.

Find a base line, preferably one boundary of the yard, and construct a line perpendicular to it to establish the grid.

Establish and plot locations of boundaries and major landmarks.

3. Measure each stone from two fixed points such as a wall or a building. Plot each stone on the map.

A numerical system may be used to identify individual stones; this may be further refined by dividing the graveyard into blocks identified by letter. The stones may then be located by block letter and individual number.

In a large yard, proceed by mapping one block at a time, using the largest format that is comfortable to work with. Then coordinate all blocks to create a full graveyard map and reduce the size of the entire map to provide a graveyard overview. For study or location of stones, the individual block maps may be used.

A simple system of symbols to denote types of monuments may also be helpful in preparing the map.

4. Provide cross-referencing by name of deceased so stones can be located in the yard both numerically an alphabetically.

5. A particularly complex graveyard may benefit from mapping by a professional surveyor.

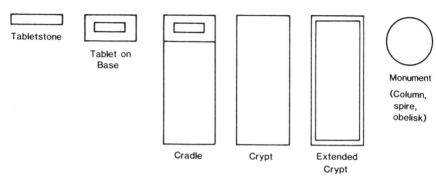

Figure 10. Symbols such as these for types of gravemarkers are useful in preparing a graveyard map. Drawing by Carol Perkins.

individuals who want to locate specific stones. With the extensive effort that a complete graveyard document represents, the document should be put to good use, and that requires that it be both secure and available.

An accurate document of an old yard serves many uses. It clearly establishes that the yard exists, which protects it from encroaching buildings, roads, and other development. It identifies the stones that belong there and their positions in the yard. This assists serious researchers and also the general public in their study and appreciation of the yard. It makes it possible to identify a marker taken from the yard. And it makes possible the use of the best conservation methods, in both a current preservation project and those that may follow many years hence.

Surveys of a number of graveyards recorded citywide, countywide, or even statewide or provincewide may also be available in some areas. Where such surveys exist, a summary of the documentation of a newly inventoried yard and information regarding where to obtain detailed information for that yard should become a part of the comprehensive survey (see appendix B for sample form).

Archaeology

The importance of an archaeological survey is often overlooked at the time a graveyard preservation project is contemplated. This is unfortunate because a community's ancient burial ground may be the oldest relatively undisturbed land for miles around, and as such, it may yield important archaeological data.

An archaeological survey does not imply "digging up the graveyard," as some may fear. Initially, a sampling is taken, under the direction of an archaeologist, to determine if there are any significant features that should be explored. What archaeologists hope to find includes foundations of earlier structures, metal, pottery, and china shards, indicating the kinds of activity that might have gone on at the site in an earlier day. Sometimes the perimeter of a graveyard is a rich source of information, revealing remains of neighboring buildings or activities.

From the sampling, the archaeologist will be able to ascertain whether a more thorough survey is warranted, and a decision must be made whether to proceed. If the area is a particularly sensitive one, if it is dense with gravestones, for instance, and the local community opposes any exploration there, the sampling is documented and no further excavation need follow.

Once a preservation project has disturbed the ground through the uprooting of trees, the resetting of stones, or the laying of new foundations for monuments, the site may be of little use to archaeologists. Their information is gained by examining undisturbed soil, a layer at a time, to determine the timeframe of the clues they find to past cultures. You cannot, therefore, plan to go back and have an archaeological survey made after the preservation project is completed.

An interesting archaeological feature found in some areas of the country are post molds. A post mold is the imprint remaining after a wood post has disintegrated or been removed and its hole has filled with earth or decayed matter. These molds are sometimes discernible long after the posts are gone. In some early settlements grave rails—two wood posts and a crosspiece that spanned the length of the grave—commonly preceded stone markers. Working in an old burying ground, a careful observer may recognize a post mold of one of these grave rails while cutting away a shovelful of earth. The vertical cross-section of the post mold could be U-shaped and from twelve to eighteen inches deep. The same mold seen in horizontal cross-section would probably be circular and about three or four inches in diameter. Finding such a formation, or any other unusual formations, should alert the layman to check with an archaeologist before proceeding with work on the site. Many unrecorded grave sites may be found through the discovery of post molds, and archaeologists will want to examine the molds to learn what types of material compose them.

Expense is one reason archaeological surveys are often bypassed in making graveyard preservation plans. While it is true that archaeological surveys can be costly, it is possible that a state can provide an archaeologist's services on a limited basis or can refer a group to possible sources for obtaining funds. Or an archaeologist may be willing to take a sampling as a contribution to a preservation project, or to make a limited survey as an education project connected with a university program.

In any case, do not sell short the importance of an archaeological survey. Check out all possible resource people and plan to make at least a sampling as part of the overall project. For information about a brochure on this subject, see the Sources of Additional Information in the back of this book.

4

REMEDIES

Cleaning and Maintaining the Site

Good maintenance is the basic preservation procedure. When neglect has been longstanding and the damage is severe, when the site is badly overgrown and there are broken stones and fragments lying about, the situation is critical, and responsible action should be taken without delay.Ideally, documentation of the entire yard should take place before clean-up. If this is not feasible, be sure *no fragment is moved prior to documentation.*

Simply cleaning up a neglected yard can sometimes transform it from a public embarrassment into an object of civic pride. Moreover, an area that is neat and well cared for is less likely to become the meeting place of vandals or the refuge of derelicts. For these reasons, then, and because the cleaning up of grounds is work that can effectively use the services of volunteers, an organized clean-up effort generates public support for the yard's well-being and for the overall preservation project. Some common mistakes and problems, however, often accompany well-intended but uninformed clean-up projects. (See figures 11, 12, 13, 14.)

If the graveyard needs just a simple clean-up, the job may require nothing more than finding, scheduling, and supervising a group of volunteers. You may be able to work effectively though civic volunteer groups such as the Boy Scouts; through business associations such as the Elks Club or Junior League; through a church group, historical society, or local graveyard association. Be forewarned, however, that sustaining a permanent maintenance crew of unpaid volunteers requires responsible supervision, constant vigilance, and periodic injections of enthusiasm, not to mention money for equipment and its proper care. Citizens who would be happy to donate rakes and shovels and mowing and trimming equipment for a one-shot, all-out effort may not feel the same about providing equipment for permanent maintenance. A

43

A.

B.

Figure 11. Maintaining the site. (A) An unkempt yard invites vandals. (B) Neglect leads finally to total disintegration of stones and destruction of historic graveyards. Photographs by Daniel Farber.

A.

B.

Figure 12. A vandalized stone before and after vandalism. Destruction of stones by vandals is increasing. This soul effigy has been used for target practice. (John Holyoke, 1775, Newton, Massachusetts.) Photographs by Harriette Merrifield Forbes and Daniel Farber.

Figure 13. Dislocated stones. These stones are no longer gravemarkers for they no longer mark graves. At best, they are memorials, something less than their intended function. Considerable information is lost when a stone is moved from its original location; it is also more vulnerable to theft and destruction. Photograph by Daniel Farber.

strong leader is needed to ensure continuing interest if a permanent volunteer crew is expected to carry out an established maintenance schedule.

Cleaning and maintaining a neglected, overgrown graveyard may also involve some bureaucratic considerations. The maintenance responsiblities may be the jurisdiction of the city, so that improvements require the cooperation of the city maintenance department or another city department, such as the department for parks and recreation. Sometimes, if the yard is already fairly well maintained, a carefully placed suggestion concerning appropriate maintenance for historic graveyards can be effective. At the same time, bear in mind that the maintenance of an old yard can be subject to sudden and drastic changes resulting from changes in maintenance personnel or funds. Anyone considering funding for improved maintenance will want to do some

Figure 14. A result of poor grounds maintenance. Trees allowed to grow haphazardly in graveyards often envelop nearby stones. (Isaac Rice, Meriden, Connecticut.) Photograph by Daniel Farber.

thinking beyond the project itself so that the results of the work will not begin to deteriorate as soon as the crews have departed.

Good maintenance does not necessarily imply a manicured appearance; indeed, an old yard's atmosphere may be enhanced by a relaxed but controlled growth of wildflowers and grasses. If close mowing and trimming is preferred, be sure the caretaker knows how to avoid damaging the stones and is supplied with equipment that makes it possible to do so. Rubber bumpers placed on power mowers, for example, help to protect stones from mower damage (these can be fashioned from discarded inner tubes). Using nylon whip grasscutters ("weedeaters") for close trimming is another, better, protective measure. Be sure a blade guard is on the mower; it protects not only the markers from sticks and rocks thrown by the mower but it protects passers-by as well.

Of course, even these measures may not be enough to protect particularly soft stones such as soapstone or any unstable stone. Grass around such stones should be clipped by hand. Low groundcovers such as clovers can eliminate the need for trimming altogether in such cases or in hard-to-reach places or areas dense with stones (see also the section on landscaping, below). Riding lawnmowers are inappropriate for use in early graveyards, since these yards generally have closely set stones, and riding mowers cannot be precisely enough controlled to ensure that stones are not damaged (figure 15).

Do not use commercial herbicides near gravestones. Virtually all contain salts or acids that are damaging to most stone, particularly marble and limestone. Fertilizers may also be acidic and should be used sparingly.

Be sure the caretaker has adequate instructions for reporting problems, including broken stones and fragments. Any caretaker should be made aware of the importance of fragments and of the immediate location in which each is found. If there is a storage facility available, make sure that instructions as to how stones are to be stored are clear and stress the importance of documenting any stone fragment before moving it.

Another important consideration to remember in graveyard clean-up is that shrubs and trees can be replaced; old stones cannot. Many fine old gravestones have been lost because tree roots grew around them or dislodged them from their locations. The trunk of a young tree growing near a stone can in time envelop it. The roots of overgrown vines penetrate and damage early brickwork and soft stone such as marble and sandstone. Dense foliage can keep stones, particularly sandstone, damp enough to accelerate their deterioration. A rule of thumb to follow is, when in doubt, remove the foliage (See figure 14.)

As with all rules, there are exceptions. One might consider moving a stone rather than taking down a 500-year-old live oak, for example, or a shrub brought from Europe by a philanthropist seventy-five years ago, the last time the graveyard received much attention. In such cases, the plantings, too, play an important part in the graveyard's history. But be conservative with exceptions: do not move stones from their original sites capriciously. If their current location is their original one, it is historically significant. Once a stone is moved, it is no longer a gravemarker, for it no longer marks a burial site. It is instead a memorial marker that does not show family and other relationships that may have been evident when the stone was in its original location. A moved stone alters the historic graveyard.

As part of cleaning and maintaining the graveyard, two conveniences should be provided for visitors: trash receptacles and benches. By doing so, you offer an alternative to littering and to resting on stones. Be sure, also, to arrange for trash receptacles to be emptied regularly so that they will not become one more maintenance problem.

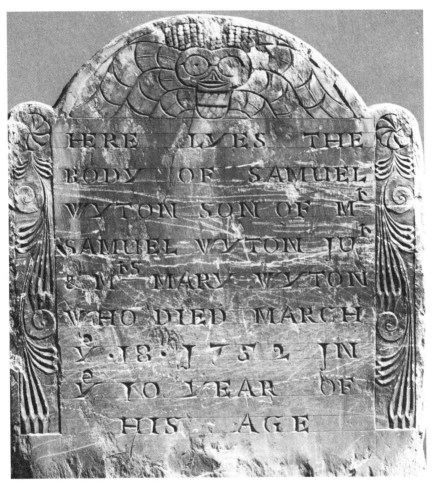

Figure 15. Lawnmower damage. Probably the greatest threat to historic stones in maintained yards is the power mower, which nicks, scars, and sometimes breaks through the protective outer layer of markers. (Samuel Wyton, 1752, South Hingham, Massachusetts.) Photograph by Daniel Farber.

Figure 16. Document fragments. All stones and fragments should be documented before they are moved. Photograph by Daniel Farber.

Basic Do's and Don'ts of Graveyard Maintenance

Don't mow immediately next to stones. Do use a nylon whip ("weedeater") for close trimming.

Do equip the mower with a rubber guard and blade guard.

Don't use commercial herbicides around stones.

Do plant small, close-lying clovers and groundcovers near stones and in other hard-to-mow areas.

Do remove scrub trees and prune shrubs to prevent damage to stones.

Don't move stones capriciously (to make straight rows for easier mowing, to create paths, or to "correct" a stone's facing orientation).

Do provide trash receptacles and benches. Do have the bins emptied regularly.

Do use signs to inform visitors of regulations.

Do educate the maintenance personnel regarding procedures for historic graveyard care.

Caring for Stone Fragments

Stone fragments are vulnerable to theft by collectors and thoughtless souvenir-hunters; to damage by vandals and power mowers; to discard by ill-informed clean-up crews; to damage by visitors who may step on them; to displacement if they are placed in a church or historical society basement for "safekeeping" (figure 16). Chances are that even inside a church basement they will in time become unidentifiable and will eventually be discarded. Perhaps this year's sexton knows where all those stone bits came from, but will he be in charge in five years? In twenty? And even the best memory is subject to loss regarding details. What then is the best way to store fragments until a major conservation project is under way?

The ideal procedure is to document each fragment and store it, clearly and securely identified, in a safe, dry place. Securing safe storage for stone parts is an important part of a graveyard preservation project, particularly if conservation work cannot begin immediately. Such storage requires a permanently available repository that will house large, broken stones and fragments in such a way that they can be effectively cataloged and easily retrieved when the time comes for their repair. Dry air is best for the stones and for the preservation of the identification tags attached to them.

When yard clean-up takes place, and *before any fragment is moved,* make a clear and accurate catalog of each broken or dislodged stone and of each fragment. Identify fragments with respect to the graveyard (or other location), the location within the graveyard in which each was found, and the headstone (by name) to which each belongs, if this can be determined. A photograph and a sketch of existing pieces should be kept with the documentation sheet for each gravestone. Pieces known to be missing should also be documented. A dislodged stone should be similarly cataloged by the location in which it was found, even though later on in the project clues could lead to identification of its proper graveyard location. Unidentifiable fragments, too, should be labeled according to the locations in which they are found. No fragments or bricks should be discarded, no matter how unimportant they may seem to be; sometimes a jigsaw puzzle comes together after much time. In cataloging, be sure not only that all fragments are listed but also that the fragments themselves are identified with a secure but removable identification mark.

In a graveyard containing many broken or dislodged stones, logistics and funds may preclude treating all stones in an ideal manner. In such cases, the most historically and artistically significant stones, those that pose a safety threat to visitors or to other stones, and those in the more advanced states of deterioration should be selected and dealt with as indicated in the following paragraphs.

Although permanent removal of a stone from its original site must be regarded as a serious action acceptable only in extreme circumstances relating to the preservation of a particularly significant stone, temporary removal (or, better still, movement to an indoor location at the site) for protection of the stone until such time as conservation can take place is highly appropriate and responsible after considering the following factors.

One satisfactory solution is to house the selected stone indoors in a simple wooden case (with no top, or, if necessary, a raised top that allows passage of air and water vapor while protecting the stone from any falling objects). The case should follow the general configuration of the stone with the stone fitting loosely into the box. The stone may rest on a bed of clean graded sand (playbox sand works nicely) or on a styrofoam cushion. A one-inch sheet of styrofoam, such as that used in building insulation, works well. Styrofoam packing material is also acceptable, although its light weight and tendency to fly about make it difficult to work with. The stone, resting loosely in its bed, should be kept from undue pollutants, moisture, or freezing. No material should be used in this stone housing that will create a vapor barrier — that is, no plastic bases or coverings. A stone is best cared for when allowed to breathe freely.

Additional stones may be stored in this manner as well, but keep in mind their cumulative weight and avoid stacking any stone directly on top of another. Shelves that support each stone and provide breathing room are most satisfactory.

If all appropriate stones cannot be placed in indoor storage, the less delicate and/or significant ones may be treated in the field. To provide temporary protection for stones that cannot be removed from the field (for example, over a winter if stone conservation is to take place within the following year), a wooden shelter may be built over the stone whether it is erect or lying on the ground. The shelter may provide a roof with canvas sides, for example, to keep out snow and rain. Passage of water vapor is essential, however, so plastic is not an appropriate housing material. Another way to prevent deterioriation is to set the individual stone pieces on a slightly raised platform such as a wooden pallet that again allows for water movement while keeping the stone above the moist ground and minimizing the effects of numerous freeze-thaw cycles.

Sometimes, however, the large and substantial storage area required for storing large stone fragments, as well as the manpower and equipment for moving stones, simply is not available. In such cases, one practical solution is to document all fragments and then to bury identifiable ones behind the standing major fragment ("parent" stone) to which each belongs. Some types of stones deteriorate more slowly in the ground than when they are exposed to the pollution and harsh elements above ground; buried stones, too, are safe from theft and careless breakage and can easily be recovered at the time of a major stone conservation effort. A depth of only a few inches below grade is sufficient and makes recovery with a probe safe and easy. Unidentifiable fragments should be buried at a few carefully documented locations nearest where each was found. Remember that the same careful documentation of all buried pieces must be kept as would be done if these same pieces were removed and stored above ground.

Burying fragments for storage is an effective procedure that volunteer groups can do. First, dig a hole ten to fifteen inches deep, depending on the thickness of the stone, in which the stone can lie flat. Place about two inches of clean, graded sand in the hole for drainage and to support any irregularities in the stone. Carefully place the stone flat, face up in the sand. Cover the stone with sand, particularly if the soil is a staining variety, then add about six inches of soil and sod.

Landscaping

Seventeeth- and eighteenth-century graveyards generally were very simple, with no landscaping plans. Such sites are, of course, the easiest to maintain.

By the mid-nineteenth century, however, the rural cemetery movement arose, primarily because of overcrowding in city churchyards, which led to unhealthy conditions and a perceived need to remove the burial grounds from the cities. These Victorian cemeteries were, and are, often elaborately designed. From the entrance gates, which were seen as earthly gates to paradise, to the interior, which held an ordered sense of balance and peace, often with enclosed spaces for contemplation and broad vistas to view the sublime in nature, they were designed to lift the spirit to feel the presence of God. The original landscaping plans for such Victorian cemeteries often included elaborate plantings of flowers, shrubs, and trees, together with pathways and marked roads and avenues. To reproduce and maintain such a scheme, however, may require more labor and expense than most cemeteries in the twentieth century can afford without extensive fund-raising efforts.

The very minimal landscaping most graveyards require generally includes removing dead trees and branches that could fall and damage the markers.

It may also include removing trees whose roots or trunks are threatening to break or dislodge stones. Many stones have been destroyed by small scrub trees that either through neglect or lack of foresight have been allowed to grow into large, damaging trees. Overgrown bushes and vines that are encroaching on the markers should be either trimmed or removed.

Except for the most elaborate and truly grand cemeteries, however, additional plantings may not be needed or even appropriate. More practical, and also more appropriate for many old graveyards, is a plan that provides for groundcovers, especially in areas that are either not easily reached by lawnmowers or are too shady to sustain a cover of grass. Carefully planned use of groundcovers can be an effective method of decreasing weekly graveyard maintenance while protecting stones from potential mower damage and at the same time beautifying the graveyard. In some Victorian cemeteries, particularly the less elaborate ones and those that are finding it difficult to live up to the nineteenth-century promise of perpetual care without additional funds, groundcovers can be a practical solution to a considerable maintenance problem.

In Victorian cemeteries, the most obvious places for groundcovers often are within plots defined by low walls with coping stones. Although an essential feature of the graveyard, these borders, like the retaining walls so common in rolling Victorian cemeteries, can pose problems in maintenance. Very little regular attention need be paid to such plots once appropriate groundcovers are well established within them. Such plantings usually last many years and need only watering and fertilizing. Planting groundcovers around individual stones eliminates the need for even a nylon weed whip in regular maintenance, and when planted according to an established overall graveyard landscaping plan, they can be effective in dealing with large problem areas, including areas of greatest marker concentration. Repeated patterns of blossoming groundcover flowers at various times of the year can do much to enhance large areas of a graveyard. Suitable groundcovers that may flourish under varying conditions include small, close-lying clovers, creeping phlox, periwinkle, sedum, or grasses such as centipede grass.

Those who seek authentic vegetation for seventeenth- and eighteenth-century graveyards may observe that such a treatment is not "historically correct." While the observation is true, the response must be that the only correct vegetation for seventeenth- and eighteenth-century graveyards is often a mixture of native grasses maintained by grazing sheep and goats. The common alternative, a high-maintenance lawn cover, is expensive to maintain and may be the cause of the greatest damage to early stones in a cared-for yard. With these as the correct and popular alternatives, the mown lawn modified with carefully chosen groundcovers becomes an attractive choice.

Ideally, preparation of such a plan should be undertaken by a historical landscape architect who can recommend correct foliage choices for given conditions as well as offer an overall plan for the yard. Implementation of such a plan can begin in early stages of the project, with further development taking place over several years, if necessary.

A landscape architect is essential if you are contemplating work in a Victorian-era cemetery. A historical landscape architect may be difficult to locate, particularly an individual both sensitive to and familiar with historic graveyard plans and plantings. Still, this individual is essential if one is to maintain the historical accuracy of a complex Victorian cemetery. In selecting this professional, insist on one who will research original plans and other early information on the particular cemetery you are preserving and who is willing to work with the original plan rather than imposing a new one "in the character of" the earlier style. Such an individual can determine what was once there, as well as what may be appropriate for the cemetery of a given date.

A decision must be made as to whether the intent is to preserve what exists now or to make an attempt to restore the cemetery to what it may have looked like in an earlier era. True "restoration" amounts to turning back the hands of time and, as such, is nearly impossible in cemeteries, as in eighteenth- and nineteenth-century buildings. Graves have been added, saplings have grown into giant oaks, and another five acres may have been added to the rear of the cemetery. Given such circumstances, the best approach often is to preserve what is presently there. Such a guideline suggests leaving as much of the earlier-era plantings as possible while replacing appropriate areas with foliage similar to what had been planted in earlier years.

In some cases, changes over time, costs, or other considerations may require deviating from an original plan, but such changes should always be made as informed choices. Where no original plan exists, and where any early information regarding a particular cemetery is scant, the plan of a similar nearby cemetery, especially one by the same architect, may yield details appropriate to the cemetery being preserved. Such adaptations are appropriate only when direct information regarding the cemetery in question is unavailable. Avoid twentieth-century hybrids and avoid romanticizing the plan to suit modern views of what a nineteenth-century cemetery looked like. Retaining historical accuracy is of primary importance, and the selection of a historical landscape architect should reflect this view.

Even in simpler, earlier graveyards, a landscape architect can tell which existing trees and shrubs are healthy or valuable and which are not. A professional can select trees and shrubs that need pruning or removal. Such an
individual can also oversee pruning crews, ensuring that no stones are damaged
in that process. A professional can develop a landscape plan that is appropriate
for an old graveyard and in keeping with the financial resources available.
In developing the plan, the landscape architect can help you make choices
that consider not only the cost of implementing the plan but also the cost
of future maintenance, designating plantings that will perform best in specific
areas and that will complement each other overall.

Unfortunately, when funds run short the landscape architect is often the
first professional to be crossed off the list. If funds simply do not permit
employment of a professional to plan and implement the landscaping, try
to engage a landscape architect informally or on a short-term basis for sound
suggestions and possible admonitions. If the budget does not permit even
this, perhaps an amateur horticulturist may be willing to give assistance. At
the very least, be sure any pruning crew working in the yard understands
the importance of the stones and has the skills to avoid damaging them.
Improper pruning can do more damage than none at all. Avoid, too, the
common mistake of beginning landscaping improvement (a step beyond clean-
up) before stone conservation is completed. In many cases crypts have to be
rebuilt, stones reset, or other procedures undertaken, any of which would
disturb previous landscaping efforts.

Finding a Gravestone Conservation Professional

Extensive efforts may be needed to find a professional familiar with gravestone conservation. There are very few available because the field of conservation and restoration of early historic graveyards is new and has not yet
attracted many qualified professionals as consultants or contractors. Masonry
contractors sometimes specialize in restoration of eighteenth- and nineteenth-
century stone or brick work, but these, too, are few. Given the state of the
art, the most experienced and best qualified professionals are quick to admit
to problems in treating ancient stones and structures. For many of these problems, time-tested solutions have not yet been developed.

Keep in mind that masons familiar with new construction may not be familiar with early construction techniques or with the problems and conditions
common to old, hand-cut stone. Methods of restoration and conservation
of these early structures and stones differ from methods used for modern

work. Conservation is extremely time-consuming work, often with variables not readily apparent at the onset of a project. Each stone's repair amounts to custom work. Contractors who work primarily with new construction are generally unfamiliar with and often reluctant to take on work of this nature as are many dealers in the monument trade. Generally speaking, their equipment and their staffs are not set up to handle ancient, fragile artifacts. The lowest bid is not the major criterion, either. Examine carefully and in detail what that low-bid figure represents.

Word of mouth recommendations may be the most accurate guideline in choosing a professional. Who repaired your neighbor's 1798 brick kitchen fireplace? Who repaired your historical society's nineteenth-century limestone urns and marble fireplace mantel? Do you know of any gravestone conservation work that you can inspect? When was it done? What methods were used? Was there a written report to which you might refer? Who did the work? How does it look to you? Are those who paid for the work satisfied? Would you be satisfied with similar work?

Compile a list of professionals whose work is as closely related to gravestone conservation as possible. You may gain assistance in your search from your state or local historical society, state historic preservation officer, local preservation foundation, architectural preservation firms, nearby universities, museums, or the modern monument industry. Remember that the interests of any of these groups may not entirely coincide with yours. A museum conservator, for example, may not be familiar with stonemasons in the area but might direct you concerning proper stone-cleaning techniques. Some monument dealers may suggest cutting new stones to replace old, since new work is their primary orientation, while others may be sensitive to the issues surrounding historic gravestone restoration. A cemeterian may offer valuable assistance regarding grounds maintenance as it relates to graveyard preservation. In looking over the Sources of Additional Information at the back of this book, note the types of firms represented. Even if the listed firms are not in your locale (they may or may not be willing to travel), they nevertheless suggest directions in which to extend your search for the right professionals. Be imaginative. Then check the references of the professionals suggested to you; talk with their former clients; look critically at their work. Slowly you will compile a list of professionals with such titles as conservator, masonry preservation consultant, masonry contractor, restoration brick/stone contractor, masonry restoration artisan, and occasionally, graveyard preservation consultant, gravestone conservation specialist, or gravestone conservator. Give particular attention to those individuals who recognize the importance of a preliminary condition report concerning the graveyard and who offer to prepare a final report upon completion of the project.

Following are general categories of professionals and what to expect from each:

• *Consultants* make recommendations concerning requirements and specifications for the work to be done. A consultant may be a working consultant who will direct volunteers when appropriate and oversee a masonry contracting crew. Others provide specifications only.

• *Conservators* are often associated with museums. They can prepare recommendations as well as undertake the stone conservation work. Some conservators deal only with indoor work and may not be familiar with the problems of exterior stone. Architectural conservators, though still few in number, are usually well equipped to deal with the field problems of gravestone conservation.

• *Contractors* (restoration contractors) may work to the specifications of a consultant or may provide their own recommendations, depending on their background and experience.

• *Scientists* (conservation scientists) develop new technologies in stone conservation. Some may be willing to repair selected stones.

Steer clear of:

• *Anyone who makes the job sound quick and easy.* In nearly all cases, it is slow, painstaking, and complicated work. Most stones will never look "like new," although it may take a careful eye to discern a quality repair.

• *Coatings.* Most coatings available in the United States today form a film on the surface of the stone that is impermeable to water vapor. Such "protective coatings" prevent the passage of water within and beyond the surface of the stone and will do more harm than good in the long run. A few water repellents are currently available that allow passage of water vapor within and beyond the stone. Such formulations may be appropriate for gravestones, but a professional stone conservator should advise you about their use.

• *Sandblasting and high-pressure water blasting* to clean stones. Only under a conservator's carefully controlled specifications is abrasive blasting of any sort appropriate for cleaning early stonework. (In a few instances, pressure cleaning with micro-fine particles is used by museum conservators to clean certain decorative elements. Museum conservators, however, are not often available for general graveyard conservation.) A commercial stone-cleaning company that uses blasting is not appropriate for cleaning ancient gravemarkers. Sandblasting removes the top layer of brick or stone, exposing a new, often softer layer to the atmosphere, hastening its deterioration. Even very hard stone is pitted by the blasting process, exposing a greater surface area to the detrimental effects of weathering and pollution. Water blasting can be as dangerous. Generally pressure should not exceed ninety pounds per square inch (psi) for most early stones. That is less pressure than a strong spray from a garden hose nozzle, and even so is more pressure than some of these delicate stones can tolerate.

•*Chemical cleaning agents.* In most cases, a gentle scrubbing with a mild, non-ionic detergent and water is best for early gravestones.

•*Recarving stone.* When early stones are recarved, the result is the work of a late-twentieth-century carver. The best plan is to document the epitaph carefully, photograph the marker, and apply appropriate conservation measures to maintain the life of the stone as long as possible.

•*Anyone who suggests removing stones and recasting them* as an ideal solution, or one to be given equal consideration with other conservation measures. This is an extreme solution, although there are occasions when this procedure is advisable (see the section on removal of stones later in this chapter).

In summary, look for:

•A professional who comes highly recommended. Check references.
•A professional whose work you have seen.
•A professional who has had experience with aged and fragile stone.
•A professional who understands the characteristics of stone and is willing to take the time necessary for the nature of the work.
•A professional who admits to not having all the answers concerning stone conservation.
•A professional who offers to produce a final report.

The most cost-effective approach to gravestone repair and graveyard preservation occurs when a team of preservation professionals works in conjunction with a concerned church or community group in a well-funded effort, undertaking the entire conservation process at one time. If this approach is not possible, the repair of designated stones can proceed until funds allow the completion of the entire project. If there is a possibility that you may have to interrupt or extend the work period while raising additional funds, be sure to discuss this with the professionals you choose, to see if they are able to work under these conditions and whether or not it will affect their cost estimates.

It is a good idea, too, to prepare a list of stones that have been chosen for repair. A carefully prepared list will provide clarification for all concerned and will avoid the misunderstandings and confusion that can result if the conditions of the stones change during the course of the project. The selection of the stones to be given immediate repair is a crucial step. Factors to consider in making the selection are the relative condition of the markers; the relative historic or artistic importance of various threatened stones; the funds available compared with the total cost; and whether or not additional funds will be needed — or forthcoming. See appendix C for a selected list of conservation professionals.

Cleaning Old Gravestones

At this point, the philosophical question of whether or not to clean old gravemarkers arises. There are those who fear the stones will look "like new" and that their early graveyard will lose its character if the stones are cleaned. The concern is not well founded, however, because there is character in the rich variety of shapes, materials, and carving styles of the early stones. Cleaning can reveal beautiful stone characteristics such as the striations of marble, as well as lettering obscured by pollutants and dirt. It can give the graveyard an uplifted, cared-for appearance. In addition, most stones in need of repair must be cleaned in order to approximate a color match in the repair.

On the other hand, serious damage can be done to stones by the use of improper cleaning methods. Not all stones can be safely cleaned, even if they appear to be stable. Even the most careful procedures have in some instances caused damage to surface texture and consequently to the lettering and decorative carving.

Staining and obscuring of lettering and inscriptions on stones is generally caused by a number of types of biological growth together with surface soiling such as that caused by atmospheric pollution and airborne soiling agents. Fungi, lichens, and algae flourish in damp, shady areas on stones, explaining frequent heavy soiling and staining on stones under large trees, adjacent to heavy foliage or with vines growing on them, and near ground level. Such biological growth appears in many colors, some remains of which may be evident even after serious cleaning efforts. Much of this growth is acidic in nature, actually etching the surface of marble and limestone gravemarkers in addition to discoloring them.

Atmospheric pollution deposited on stones originates primarily from exhaust from automobiles and industry. In addition to causing carbonaceous deposits, atmospheric pollution carries sulfur dioxide, which, when in contact with water, produces the distressingly familiar acid rain, another particularly destructive force on marbles and limestones. In porous stones, airborne particles, whether from exhaust, soil, or plants and animals, settle into the pores, leaving surface deposits that in time become difficult to remove.

Apparently a simple procedure, cleaning nevertheless requires care, some instruction, and some familiarity with stones. Although in many cases effective work may be carried out by volunteers and regular maintenance staff without benefit of on-site training, it is strongly advised that, even with outlined procedures, actual work take place only after an on-site training program led by a graveyard preservation professional. An on-site professional can identify stones that cannot be safely cleaned and can supervise the cleaning of those stones that require it, either providing a trained crew or training and supervising volunteers.

No stone should be cleaned if its stability is questionable — a stone with its face or lettering flaking, with significant fractures, with a grainy surface that readily falls away, or with any other condition that indicates that the stone is delicate, brittle, or otherwise vulnerable.

After selecting a stable stone to be cleaned, remove loose dry materials with a soft-bristled brush. Then test-clean a small, unnoticeable area by going through the entire cleaning process (as outlined below) in that area. This test will alert a careful observer to problems that may arise in cleaning the whole stone, will give an indication of effective cleaning solutions, and will give an idea of the results that may be expected as well.

Clean stones by first wetting them thoroughly with clear water, then scrubbing with soft-bristled brush and plain water (use a brush with tampico — natural — or plastic bristles, never wire). Always clean a stone from the bottom up to avoid streaking. After the initial flooding and scrubbing with water only, use cleaning solutions for a given type of stone as indicated on the chart below. Pre-wet the stone before using each cleaning agent; then apply cleaning agent and scrub. After using each cleaning agent, flood the stone thoroughly and scrub again with clean water. Do not allow any cleaning solution to dry on the stone prior to removing it.

In most cases, a solution of a mild, non-ionic detergent (such as Igepal or Triton-X 100, available through conservators' supply houses) and water is effective in loosening and removing most or all surface dirt. Photo-Flo is another such cleaning agent and is usually available locally through photographic supply houses. Household ammonia may be effective on marble and limestone. Do not make the common mistake, however, of assuming that other common cleaning agents are acceptable for cleaning most types of stones; in most cases, they are not. Select cleaning agents from the chart in order to avoid introducing damaging materials into the stones.

A soft, wooden stick such as an ice cream stick or tongue depressor (never a metal instrument) may be used to clean out recesses on stone such as granite or slate. This procedure, however, can be extremely harmful to soft grainy stones such as sandstone or limestone and even to harder stones that have deteriorated. For softer stones, a cotton swab or a soft toothbrush may be effective for cleaning crevices.

After cleaning, thoroughly rinse stones with plenty of clear water. The prewetting procedure before and the rinsing procedure after cleaning are essential to prevent solutions from penetrating deeply into the stone, which could leave a residue within the stone and possibly create salting or other problems later on.

Sometimes deep-set stains remain in spite of diligent cleaning efforts. Some may be removed with poultices or other methods not outlined here. Many of these stains are difficult to remove and require processes generally better left to conservators. In all but a few cases, these stains will not seriously deface the stone and will not look out of place among the aged stones. If necessary, a conservator may be called in to perform this skilled work.

Cleaning should not be frequently repeated, as particles of stone are washed away in even the most careful cleaning procedure.

Tips on Gravestone Cleaning for Volunteers

PROCEDURES TO AVOID:
- Avoid acidic cleaners on marble or limestone.
- Avoid sandblasting gravestones.
- Avoid high-pressure spraying.
- Do not attempt to clean any stone that is unstable.
- Do not attempt to clean stones without first receiving proper direction.
- Never use wire brushes or any metal instrument in cleaning stone.
- Do not substitute household cleaners for those listed here.
- Do not clean stones often. Even the most carefully cleaned stone loses stone particles with each cleaning. Do not plan to clean stones more often than once every several years, or longer.
- Avoid treating stones with "protective" coatings that are impermeable to water vapor. Such coatings can actually be very harmful to stones in years to come, and others are ineffective.

TOOLS FOR STONE CLEANING:
- Plastic pails
- Goggles
- Rubber gloves

- Tampico (natural bristle) or plastic scrub brushes
- Toothbrushes
- Smooth wooden sticks such as ice cream sticks or tongue depressors
- Q-tips
- Spray bottles
- Water source (a hose is helpful)

RECOMMENDED CLEANING SOLUTIONS (Listed in order of increasing strength)

Note: Always use the weakest cleaning agent that cleans stone effectively. Do not increase recommended strength of a given solution. Use only those solutions recommended for the type of stone being cleaned.

Marble and Limestone
- Water only
- Non-ionic detergent, such as Photo-Flo (available from photographic supply houses), Triton-X 100 or Igepal (available from conservators' supply houses), and water. Use 1 ounce to 5 gallons of water.
- Vulpex (a soap appropriate for stone cleaning available from conservators' supply houses) and water. Use 1 part Vulpex to 2–4 parts water.
- Household ammonia. Use 1 cup to 4 cups water.
- Calcium hypochlorite. Use only to remove biological growth. Available as swimming pool disinfectants. Use 1 pound dry to 4 gallons of water. Must be dissolved in warm water.

Soapstone
- Water only

Slate
- Water only
- Non-ionic detergent and water (see Marble).

Sandstone
- Water only
- Non-ionic detergent and water (see Marble).

Resetting Old Gravestones

Large tablestones have a tendency to sink into the ground with the passage of time. Many sink enough to obscure part of their inscriptions. Occasionally, a sunken headstone, showing only a few inches above ground, appears to be a footstone. To read inscriptions, then, and to prevent losing some stones altogether, resetting is sometimes necessary.

Figure 17. Resetting. This slate stone, in danger of falling due to its own weight, is in need of resetting. Note the carver's signure, "J. New," intended to be underground. (Gardner Waters, 1793, Sutton, Massachusetts.) Photograph by Daniel Farber.

Ideally, the resetting of early gravestones should be done by a stone conservation professional working with a professionally trained crew. Still, resetting can sometimes be effectively carried out by trained volunteers and regular maintenance staff. While in many cases effective work may be accomplished by untrained volunteers following outlined procedures, it is strongly advised that on-site training be given before actual work takes place, as indicated earlier.

Is Resetting Necessary?

Only a stone whose inscription is markedly obscured by its sunken state or a stone at risk of being broken because of its extreme lean should be considered for resetting (figure 17). Stones should never be reset simply to straighten a minor tilt or to line them up in straight rows. It is possible that a stone facing a direction different from its neighbor has been reset and reversed at some time in the past.

It was common practice in the seventeenth and eighteenth centuries to bury the dead in an east-west orientation, so that on the Day of Judgment the dead would rise to face the east, since the righteous, it was believed, would be judged in the morning of that last day. The headstone and footstone were commonly set so that their inscriptions faced away from the grave. The carved face of the headstone, therefore, faced west, and that of the footstone east. There were many exceptions to this east-west positioning, however.

In the seventeenth and eighteenth centuries, a grave was often marked by both a headstone and a footstone, but to simplify mowing, many footstones have been reset close to and behind their headstones. Unfortunately, many footstones have been discarded altogether and, almost as unfortunately, some "restorers" have failed to distinguish between headstones and footstones, lining all markers in straight lines and indiscriminately separating the pairs.

But the present setting of a stone not now in its original position is also a part of the yard's history, and its present position may even have an as yet unknown significance. Do not destroy evidence that may be significant to future researchers. If, after careful consideration, you decide that you must reset some stones, carefully document the changes, stone by stone.

Is Resetting Practical?

Once a decision has been made that resetting a stone is appropriate, another consideration is whether it is wise to take the risk. If a stone moderately in need of resetting breaks in the resetting process, a major repair problem has been created. Thus, if a stone appears to be fragile, the procedure may be better left undone. If the stone is particularly valuable historically or artistically, resetting should clearly wait for the expertise of a carefully chosen professional.

Many stones contain internal fractures that are not apparent even to a careful observer. When these stones are jarred from the positions they may have held for two hundred years, they are prone to break at the fracture with the lightest blow or any sudden stress.

Slate stones that appear to be sound probably are sound and are better candidates than either marble or sandstone for resetting. Even slate, though, should be tested for soundness. If the foliated layers of stone are separating at the top, if a light tap of the finger on the face produces a hollow sound in spots, or if the face is visibly pulling away from the rest of the stone, the stone is unsound and resetting it is risky.

Marble stones are subject to interior fractures, although, like slate, most that appear to be stable truly are.

Sandstones are particularly deceptive. These stones, too, are subject to interior fractures. Their considerable vulnerability is due in large part to their porous nature and susceptibility to moisture absorption, and to such conditions as rising damp and freeze-thaw deterioration.

Granite is the hardest and the most stable gravestone material. Because of its hardness and because the early quarrying and stonecarving were done by hand, granite was both difficult to obtain and to work. As a result, there are comparatively few granite stones that date back to the seventeenth and eighteenth centuries. The majority of granite gravestones are in later cemeteries and bear late-nineteenth-century and twentieth-century dates. Many of these may be appropriately reset by a modern monument company.

Whatever its apparent condition, every early gravestone should be treated as though it were fragile. Most are. Most were cut from softer stone to begin with and have become brittle with age and exposure to the elements. In some cases the part of the stone that is at grade level has become especially weakened through rising damp and repeated freeze-thaw cycles.

Once you have selected stones for resetting and are ready to begin digging, proceed with caution. Remove earth from the back side (the uncarved side) of the marker only, if at all possible. Keeping shovels away from the carved side eliminates the possibility of marring the face of the stone. If a stone is seriously out of plumb, however, and leaning backward, it may have to be dug on the side away from the tilt, even though that is the face side. In either case, keeping the earth firm on one side provides a strong, compacted earth face against which to reset the stone.

Bear in mind that these stones are very heavy. In most cases you must expect to find as much stone below the ground as above. If the stone has sunken deep into the ground, expect more below than above, especially in the case of slate markers. This means that a marker five feet high, as some are, may extend another five feet below the ground. Calculate the weight at between 160 and 180 pounds per cubic foot, and you will find that a normally proportioned stone five feet high can easily weigh more than 500 pounds. Most tabletstones can be successfully eased out of their setting by two to four strong people, but raising others requires the use of ropes and two-by-fours working as bars and levers, much as was done by eighteenth-century craftsmen. Make sure the raising devices do not work against the stone to exert a pressure that could snap the stone before it is out of the ground. Once the stone is out, lay it gently on level ground so that it is firmly and evenly supported and out of the way of other work. Examine the stone for any additional marks such as a carver's signature, quarry marks, or sample lettering sometimes found on below-ground sections of stone. These, or any other items of interest, should be recorded both in the written document and photographically.

To help a reset marker stay in place, prepare a bed for the butt of the stone to rest on. The butts of most slate stones are pointed; marble and sandstone markers are more likely to be relatively squared-off at the bottom. The supporting bed on which the butt will be set should distribute the weight of the stone evenly, so that if any settling occurs, no serious shifting will occur with it. This bed can be of brick, which is inexpensive and readily available. Use no mortar; place level, dry-laid brick to the point where the stone will be supported and will rest at the proper level.

When preparing the bed, take care that the stone will not be set too high. This would alter the original proportions, and the balance and stability of the stone could be threatened as well. The stone itself will generally dictate the depth at which it should be reset. For example, if the epitaph is boxed in, ground level should be an inch or two below the box. If the butt of the stone is tapered, the stone usually emerges from the ground where the tapering begins. Often the butt is more roughly finished than the smooth, above-ground face, indicating where the stone should emerge from the ground. And, if the stone is signed, the carver's signature is generally the last line of carving and should show an inch or so above ground.

Before setting the stone on a brick bed, cover the brick with an inch or two of sand. This provides a cushioned surface on which the stone can rest, reducing the risk of damage to the stone.

Once the stone is in the ground, reset it against the compacted soil on

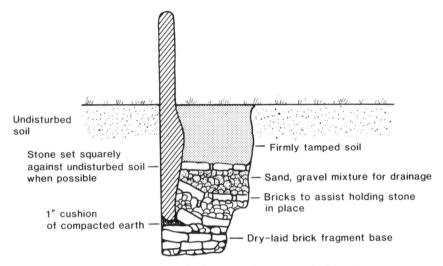

Figure 18. Resetting stones. Lay a dry fragment base covered with soil, support temporarily with brick fragments, and fill with a mixture of sand and gravel for drainage. Check for level and plumb, and fill top area with soil and sod, tamping for firm support. Drawing by Carol Perkins.

the side that was left undisturbed when the stone was removed. Then check it for level and plumb, and fill the bottom half of the cavity with a mixture of half sand and half pea gravel to facilitate drainage. Fill the remainder of the cavity with soil, tamping the soil firmly into place. Adding a little gravel or small pieces of brick may be useful in firming the setting. Place these carefully as needed, add soil, tamp, and repeat. Grade the surface to encourage drainage away from the stone (figure 18).

Although these beds can be useful in stabilizing reset stones, a good rule of thumb is: the less elaborate, the better. Most of the old tabletstones were originally set into the earth without any prepared foundation. Generally, as much stone was set below ground as is seen above, which in itself diminished the stone's tendency to lean from plumb. When in doubt, it is safe to repeat the earlier artisans' procedure. By all means, avoid overkill. For example, setting stones below grade into concrete is extremely damaging, nearly irreversible, and unsightly. In any graveyard or cemetery where the stones have been set into concrete for a few years, an observer will find many of them have snapped off at the line of the concrete (figure 19).

In spite of one's best efforts, there is no guarantee that an occasional stone will not again settle or tilt out of plumb. Many factors, such as imperfect

tamping, unusual drainage patterns, or nearby building construction can inter-
fere with the stability of a newly set stone.

Setting Incomplete Tabletstones

Some tabletstones presently consist of only one main fragment, the stone
perhaps having snapped off at ground level, the base lost long ago below
ground.

These stones pose a particular problem, since they cannot be reset in the
usual way of tabletstones, which requires nearly half the stone below ground.

A separate base into which the fragment can be set, similar to above-ground
bases found on nineteenth- and twentieth-century stones, can be made from
concrete. Setting a tabletstone in such a separate base, however, is not an
ideal solution.

*Figure 19. A preservation don't. In misguided preservation attempts, stones are fre-
quently placed in rows to simplify mowing and set into cement to keep them from
leaning. Moving the stones and setting them in cement are both ill-advised procedures. Note the number of stones that have snapped off at the cement line. Photograph by Daniel Farber.*

Setting a tabletstone into a cast base risks the emergence of problems caused by soluble salts later on. Such an occurrence is least damaging to slates, which are far less porous than other stones such as marbles or sandstones. In the more porous stones, however, soluble salts from the cast base may be wicked up into the stone, possibly causing staining and efflorescence later.

Still, when carried out as outlined below, such resetting provides an alternative to leaving fragments lying on the ground or even inside in often inadequate storage. The method is offered here, then, as an alternative, which may be considered a temporary measure to preserve stones until such time as better solutions are available.

For a model of the base into which a fragment can be set, look in the graveyard for a nineteenth-century stone that has become separated from its base. Note that the base consists of a stone block with a slot in it into which the upright tablet section of the monument is placed.

To reproduce this effect most economically, a concrete base similar to the stone models may be cast. These cast bases, however, are unlike their models in that they will rest entirely below ground, unseen once they are in place. The results are appropriate to the broken tabletstone, which originally consisted of a single piece of stone.

To make the cast base, construct a wooden box at least six inches longer than the width of the tablet (more if the tablet is exceptionally large) and at least six inches wider than the thickness. The box should be at least six to eight inches deep. Into this wooden box, pour a prepared concrete mix. This is one of the few instances where a prepared concrete mix is appropriate to early gravestone restoration.

When the bottom of the box is filled with concrete mix, a slot may be prepared in the base by adding a two-by-four plus shims to equal one quarter inch more on each of the four sides than the stone that will eventually be set into the slot. Oil the two-by-four and suspend it along the top edge of the box by attaching it to a longer support that spans the box. Fill the rest of the box with concrete mix, with the two-by-four about three inches deep into the mix.

This arrangement allows for easy removal after the mortar begins to set. When the concrete has set up just to the point where it can support its present configuration, remove the two-by-four, revealing the slot. If this is done too quickly, the slot will lose its dimensions; if it is done too late, the two-by-four will not come out without tearing the setting concrete. Let this concrete base set up for twenty-four hours; then remove the wooden form, and let the base set for several days more, undisturbed.

When the base is completely cured, a drainage bed should be prepared in the location in which the tabletstone will stand. Remove the soil, replacing it with six inches of pea gravel beneath three inches of clean sand. Then set the base into the sand, level it, and check it to see that the top edge of the base is about one and one half inches below ground level. Cover the slot to make sure no dirt or debris gets into it while you prepare the drainage bed. When you are ready to set the stone, dampen the interior of the slot in the base with water, and line the bottom and edges of the slot carefully with a 1:4:8 mortar mix (1 part white portland cement, 4 parts hydrated lime, 8 parts clean, graded sand) that is mixed fairly wet. Then insert the tabletstone into the slot, checking it for level and plumb, making corrections using wooden wedges, which will be removed before the mortar completely sets. If necessary, prop two-by-fours at each side for stability.

As the mortar starts to set, brush away any loose mortar around the edge of the stone. If the stone is still not clean, wait a couple of hours and return with a toothbrush and a spray bottle containing water to remove any remaining mortar from the stone before the mortar is set.

In some cases lettering may be unavoidably lost below ground or within the slot. Be sure the entire stone has been documented prior to this type of resetting. Check, too, for possible signatures or makers' marks near the bottom of the stone.

This technique allows fragments to be reset in the graveyard. It also is safer for the stone than setting it directly into cement. Since the setting mortar is softer than the stone, any breakage is likely to occur in the mortar, which can be replaced. Still, the potential development of efflorescence and other salting problems should be kept in mind. Common wisdom suggests that the most significant stones that are broken at the base should be stored indoors under adequate conditions until a better solution to this problem is found.

Note that this procedure is definitely *not* the same as building a box and plunking the stone into wet cement. Early gravestones should never be set into cement, as the softer, early stone types are not compatible with the much harder, modern cement. Much damage can occur in time, and the damage is always to the softer materials, in this case, the early stone.

Probing

Probing is probably the procedure most often overlooked in the course of a gravestone conservation project. It is a simple technique used to locate underground stones and fragments. Generally an iron probe (one can be fashioned from a half-inch-diameter iron rod with one end bent to resemble a cane and the other gently tapered for easy insertion into the ground) is carefully pressed into the earth at places that are likely to hold stone fragments or whole markers (figure 20). Promising locations include gaps in a row of headstones where one appears to be missing; the area above a footstone that has no corresponding headstone; the area below a headstone that has no corresponding footstone; the area behind or in front of a large standing fragment; open areas that appear to have been intrinsic parts of the burial ground; and any unmarked space where an old map of the yard shows a marker. A missing fragment from a broken stone is likely to lie where it fell, near the damaged stone that is still standing.

When the probe touches a hard object, careful digging either by hand or with a small garden trowel may uncover a marker or a fragment. Great care is required in the digging to avoid marring the surface of the buried stone. Patience is required, too, for as often as not, the uncovered piece bears no carving and is relatively unimportant or is only a brick or a bit of fieldstone.

Probing all the open areas in a large graveyard may not be feasible, but checking in likely areas can yield rich rewards. One recent conservation project in a medium-sized graveyard uncovered nineteen footstones and six headstones, all of which were either whole or repairable. Most of these were found by probing.

Monument Repair

Repair of early tabletstones, brick and stone crypts, and other monuments should be made only by qualified conservators or masonry artisans familiar with the qualities of old stone and early brick and with the special requirements of these materials and the problems they present for their repair. Special mortars, adhesives, and application techniques are used to repair these early materials that are not used when working with modern materials. Repair of early monuments should not be attempted by anyone who does not have specific skills in this area. The following information related to the various conservation processes involved in monument repair is intended only as a general introduction to certain acceptable procedures. It is offered on the premise that anyone involved with a comprehensive graveyard preservation project should have some understanding of the techniques used in order to evaluate professionals being considered for the job and to evaluate the quality of the work once it is under way. It is in no way intended as a technical step-by-step guide that will enable the layman to execute the procedures.

All repairs should be fully documented with diagrams and notes and with

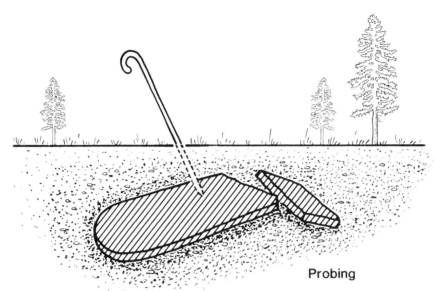

Probing

Figure 20. Probing. A probe can be fashioned from a half-inch diameter iron rod for use in locating buried stones and fragments. Drawing by Carol Perkins.

photographs made before, during, and after restoration. Review chapter 3 for a detailed description of this procedure.

A condition report should precede all conservation work. It may be as brief as a few pages in some instances, or it may be fairly extensive. It will detail the types of stones in the yard, their various forms of deterioration, their condition at the onset of the project, and the need for repair. It is essential to know exactly what problems need to be dealt with before beginning the project in order to determine how to proceed. Priorities should be determined from the material in this condition report and from information regarding the historic and artistic importance of individual stones, their prominence in the yard, and the projected cost of stabilization.

Fully documenting the work as it proceeds is important because the entries provide a complete and accurate record of repairs and changes made in the course of the project. This material fills out other documentation, providing a record of existing construction, evidence of earlier restoration or other changes, necessary twentieth-century alterations and adaptations, and the introduction of new materials. The information will be invaluable to the work of conservators of the future in their application of techniques and materials not yet developed.

In addition, the conservation professional in charge of the project should write a summary report upon completing the work. The final report outlines exactly what has taken place in the course of the project and provides a useful record for both future researchers and conservators.

Tabletstones, Especially Marble

Broken upright marble stones may be mended with threaded nylon, teflon, or stainless steel rods and polyester resin or epoxy adhesives. While nylon, teflon, and stainless steel are all acceptable repair materials, stainless steel, although strong and readily available, presents a potential problem. If it is not of a high quality, some corrosion could occur and eventually cause a staining of the stone. Teflon and nylon are recent choices of some professionals because they are inert materials that appear to be little influenced by weather or age. A few professionals have reported problems even with teflon and have turned to nylon rod. Mechanical keying to obtain an adhesive bond is necessary with both teflon and nylon, for without it the adhesive will not adhere to the rods. In some cases this may require cutting threads into the rod by hand. Teflon also poses a potential health hazard when being cut, so a protective respirator should be worn. Threaded nylon rod is readily available in most areas and is less expensive than teflon, as well.

Regarding adhesives, polyester resins have the advantage of ease of application and a reported degree of reversibility in the event a superior method of repair is developed. Epoxies, on the other hand, have a reputation for greater durability, particularly in northern areas where frequent freeze-thaw cycles can be a problem. Polyester resins and epoxies deteriorate in the presence of ultraviolet rays, such as is found in sunlight. At the least, such deterioration causes discoloration at the adhesive joint with the passage of time. To avoid a potential problem, when possible these resins should be used for interior repairs with a composite stone mix used for exterior finish work. In either case, specific formulas have been developed for use with particular types of stone. Epoxies designed for use with granite are best used with granite, for example, while polyester resins designed for use with marble are best suited for marble. Both polyester resins and epoxies present the problem of toxicity in application, so a respirator, goggles, and rubber gloves should be worn during use.

To execute this type of repair, all pieces of stone are best removed from the ground, given a preliminary cleaning, and placed on a flat work surface. Holes are then drilled to receive the rods, a delicate and exacting operation requiring skill and care to prevent further damage to fragile stone. Pins are cut to fit the holes, and the work dry-fitted with adjustments made until an exact fit is obtained. The adhesive should be pigmented to match the stone, the pins and the break then coated with adhesive, and any voids in the holes filled. The fragments should be carefully aligned and joined with clamps. Methods for cleaning up the break line vary with the adhesive used, but in all cases the best results are obtained if the line is trimmed before the adhesive is completely set. Repairs should be neat and clean, although the quality of the repair is in part dependent upon the quality of the stone being repaired, the age of the break, the degree of fragmentation, and the number of voids to be filled. Other fragments may be replaced using rods and adhesives in much the same way that major fragments are joined (figure 21).

If a large or structural fragment is missing, it may be appropriate to set in a new piece of similar marble, carved to the proper configuration, and artificially "weathered" to match the old. The new piece should be set using methods similar to those used to replace original fragments.

Composite Stone Repair

In some cases, voids can be filled with mortars that contain lime, cement, and the original stone dust, creating a simulated stone consisting of natural materials. These composite stone patching compounds must be formulated for compatibility (strength, water permeability) with a given stone type. Likewise, they must be visually satisfactory; that is, they should match the stone's color and texture. Because of the complexity of preparing an appropriate mix and the need for familiarity with successful application procedures, these mixes are generally best applied by experienced practitioners.

A few companies manufacture natural cementitious patching materials appropriate to this type of repair. Such materials have the advantages of relative ease of application and availability of mixes custom-matched to a given stone. Their chief disadvantage lies in their considerable cost.

Before any such compound is selected, however, it should be carefully examined for acceptability. Some commercial compounds, particularly those containing unknown synthetic formulations, are not compatible with the stone and are therefore not appropriate for gravestone repair.

Both small voids and larger ones can be repaired with composite stone mixes. In the case of larger voids, or perhaps with deep-relief decorative elements, an armature of threaded nylon rod, or in some cases stainless steel, may be set in place to provide additional strength to the built-up structure. Such armatures are usually set in place with the same adhesives used for set-

A.

*Figure 21. Before and after conservation of a marble headstone. (Elizabeth Peron-
neau Hayne, 1883, Charleston, South Carolina.) Photographs by the author.*

B.

ting pins in rejoining fragments. The same composite stone mix may be used to cast missing decorative elements from existing ones or to handsculpt them in place.

Large Stones

A large stone is in most cases more difficult to repair than a smaller one because of decreased maneuverability. In addition, large stones are likely to be broken in more places than small ones. The more fragments, the more complex the repair, as all fragments must be drilled to fit perfectly and should be bonded one at a time. Each successive bonding is an occasion for error because every added fragment must fit both horizontally and vertically. If you bear in mind that an error of one-sixteenth of an inch repeated in three consecutive bondings would total an error of three-sixteenths of an inch, it becomes clear that an unacceptable margin of error could all too easily occur. Moreover, stones in many early graveyards are too closely spaced to permit the use of cranes or hydraulic lifting devices. The twentieth-century craftsman is often forced to fashion custom-designed equipment or use rollers and ramps or tripods with pulley systems that approximate stone-moving devices used in the eighteenth and nineteenth centuries.

Sandstones

Sound sandstone can be repaired much as marble is repaired. Many sandstones, however, are extremely delicate and may be weak internally. These stones cannot be drilled safely, and they may present additional problems for which, at the time of this writing, there are no acceptable direct solutions.

One type of repair especially common to sandstones consists of a low viscosity cementitious grout injected between delaminating layers of stone. Such layers are generally parallel to the face of the stone and perpendicular to the ground, which allows for ease of application in place. The grout consists of lime, cement, and an especially fine graded sand mixed with water to a pourable consistency. Clay dams can be used to prevent leakage from outlets farther down the stone. Some stones show very early evidence of such delamination. In such cases, the initial procedure can be eliminated and a thicker mix matching the exterior stone visually can be used to cap the stone to prevent further water entry and provide a visually acceptable repair. Any type of stone that is delaminating may benefit from this treatment, usually familiar only to conservators.

If a deteriorated, severely threatened sandstone (or other stone) is exceptionally important historically or artistically, an alternative to giving up the stone to natural weathering and loss is to bring it indoors, preferably to a museum. Another option is to house the stone under cover in its graveyard site. Such housing is not entirely satisfactory, however. A freestanding bonnet may provide some protection, but it is aesthetically unpleasing. Other kinds of housing tend to be unacceptable because either they restrict air cir-

Figure 22. Unsuccessful preservation effort. Encased in a material harder than itself, this headstone may be deteriorating more rapidly than if it had not been treated. The treatment may have caused or may have accelerated the cracks. (Jeremiah Jewet, 1714, Rowley, Massachusetts.) Photograph by Daniel Farber.

A.

B.

C.

Figure 23. Repairing and resetting slate, before and after. The dramatic results of quality conservation work. (A and B: Charles Warhan, 1779, Charleston, South Carolina; C and D: Sarah Freer, 1760, Charleston, South Carolina.) Photographs by the author.

In Memory of
Mrs SARAH FREER wife
of Mr SOLOMON FREER
& Dau.^r of Mr SOLOMON
& Mrs AMEY LEGARE
who departed this Life
October 22.^d 1760
Aged 34 Years. & 5 M.^o

D.

culation, which is essential to the well-being of the stone, or they restrict the stone's natural rate of expansion or contraction. In any case, less is better. A hood is acceptable; encasing a stone is not. Any kind of hood should be regarded as a temporary effort, its goal being to keep the stone intact until a better method of preservation is developed (figure 22).

Slates

Slate tablets, too, may be repaired with polyester resin adhesives, although, because of slate's tendency to exfoliate, most slate stones will not accept drilling. Careful pigmentation and application of the polyester resin adhesive can result in an excellent visual repair. Long-term field testing of such repairs has not been completed, however, so monitoring and documenting this kind of repair is particularly important (figure 23).

Brick and Stone Crypts and Box Tombs

Restoring crypts and box tombs requires varying amounts of reconstruction. In many cases the total structure must be rebuilt, starting with dismantling and preparing a new footing. The rebuilt structure should duplicate the original as closely as possible. Where changes must be made, they should be described and explained in field notes and the completion report. The structure should be documented prior to dismantling, noting such elements as dimensions, brick bond, and variations. After dismantling, the interior construction and any unusual findings should be documented.

If the structure is large, such as a family vault or mausoleum, an engineer's or architect's measured drawings should document both the initial condition and any changes. In addition, an architect or historic building consultant to plan and oversee the work may also be appropriate. Work should proceed on such a structure as it would in the restoration of any historic building. Masonry artisans already involved in crypt and box tomb reconstruction are good choices for the restoration of a family vault or mausoleum. A conservator is not likely to be involved in such reconstruction unless that individual is an architectural conservator. Get separate estimates for each vault or mausoleum requiring repair, as work on each could be extensive and costly. Work on vaults and mausoleums can also be planned as separate phases of the graveyard project.

When bricks are loose or have been removed in dismantling a structure, they should be carefully cleaned and reused whenever possible. If the original exterior face is damaged, in many cases bricks can be turned around and reused. When bricks must be replaced, salvage bricks, similar in size, appearance, and composition, are a good choice. A word of warning regarding salvage bricks, however: occasionally they develop an efflorescence due to unfavorable storage conditions. If possible, check other recent applications of these bricks to see that this condition has not occurred. In some areas new replicated brick may be obtained. If enough brick is required, a particular brick type can even be custom-made to match the original brick in color, size, and texture. Replacement bricks for interiors of structures may be concrete brick, which is less expensive and more easily obtained than matching brick. Some box tomb structures include interior brick walls at each end and in the center; others do not. Such walls can be added in rebuilding in order to provide support for the slab covering the structure. The strictest interpretation regarding reconstruction does not allow the introduction of concrete brick into the integral construction of the tomb structure. The addition of such interior walls as mentioned above, however, is appropriate if they are required for strength and continued stability (figure 24).

If a brick structure requires only partial rebuilding, it should be rebuilt starting with the first course that has loose bricks. Those below should be repointed only.

Tuckpointing may be the most commonly misapplied restoration procedure in use today. Tuckpointing, like so much of restoration work, is time-consuming, labor-intensive work. Much care should be taken in removing old, loose mortar by hand, and properly applying new mortars that have been formulated for compatibility with original or existing mortars regarding color, texture, composition, and style of mortar joint. Tuckpointing should be done in accordance with the procedures outlined in articles in the United States Department of the Interior's Preservation Briefs series and in the Association for Preservation Technology's *APT Bulletin,* listed in the Sources of Additional Information at the end of this book.

Mortars of various compositions are used in the different aspects of brick and stone repair. The mortars should be compatible in strength with the brick or stone they join. A common error in masonry restoration is the use of a mortar that is harder than the elements it joins. Serious and even irremediable damage to brick and stone can occur as a result. Mortars should also approximate the color and texture of the original existing mortar. Sands vary in color and texture, and when using sand as aggregate in mortar, it is important to match it in size of grain, composition (silica, quartz, etc.), and color to that of the original mortar. Such additions as fiber and ground oyster shell may be useful in approximating an early mortar. This matching can be a complex task, requiring many samples to determine the correct mix.

Figure 24. A box tomb, before and after repair and reconstruction. All pieces are rejoined and reassembled in this restoration in Charleston, South Carolina. Photographs by the author.

The repair of a stone crypt should follow the structure's original construction, just as with a brick structure. Again, interior brick walls are occasionally added to assist in support of the crypt top. In many cases, original pins connecting the corners of marble or sandstone walls are still in place. These pins are often made of copper set in lead, and if intact, they should be reset; if not, they may be replaced with similar pins of copper or stainless steel, set with an elastic resin adhesive.

Occasionally one stone wall or a section of a stone wall is missing from a box crypt. The missing element can be recut and replaced or, perhaps simpler, bricked in, allowing a recess for a stucco surface that approximates the color and surface texture of the weathered stone. If done well, this procedure is not readily apparent visually, and it provides a structurally sound repair. It is also reversible, and if the missing piece is found, the repair can be removed and the original piece replaced in the wall.

Urgency

The urgency of making repairs cannot be overemphasized. The longer a damaged or deteriorated monument remains in disrepair, the more likely it is to become beyond repair. Some fragments may wander off with tourists and treasure seekers; fragments may be moved to a far corner of the yard where they can no longer be identified; downed stones are more vulnerable to damage from unthinking visitors, possibly through such innocent actions as stepping on fragments obscured by leaves. Once a stone or brick structure loses its structural integrity, deterioration takes place rapidly. The best course of action is to repair structures before more serious damage occurs.

Removal of Stones: A Question of Ethics

The philosophy of graveyard preservation presented throughout this book rests on the premise that good preservation and conservation measures properly applied will extend the life of gravestones and the old graveyards in which they rest. For example, I do not recommend recarving eroded inscriptions because twentieth-century carving on eighteenth-century gravestones in effect defaces a historic artifact. The alternative then is to let the old carving wear away until it is no more. The logic behind this suggests that the gravestone has served its original purpose, that of commemorating the life of the deceased for as long as the stone can tell its tale. In most cases, this is enough.

There are problems with this philosophy, however. Stone deterioriation has been greatly accelerated by acid rain and other forms of modern pollution.

Some stones are weathering away at a rapid rate. Increasingly, vandals and thieves are destroying graveyards. Clearly, other options must be found.

Much legitimate controversy exists with regard to the appropriate responses to this situation. The answers are multi-faceted and rarely definitive. With this perspective, consider the ramifications of removing an old stone from its graveyard setting.

One option for preserving markers that are particularly important and seriously threatened by their fragile condition or by their location in frequently vandalized areas is to remove them from the graveyard to indoor safekeeping. But this option is also fraught with problems.

The first consideration is who is responsible for deciding which stones should be moved and who is to be responsible for the actual procedure and care after the move. Sometimes descendants of the deceased, churches, or even caretakers feel a right and a need to remove stones for their own reasons. Art collectors, art dealers, and museums have a primary interest in the collection of historical and cultural artifacts. And municipalities may claim ownership and want to reuse the land for the economic benefit of the community. There may be legal problems with removal of gravemarkers, even for safekeeping. Some states, such as Connecticut and Massachusetts, have adopted legislation to deal with these problems. (See appendix D.)

Still, gravestones are not to be viewed as collectibles, and their acquisition by individuals or firms for private collection or sale is theft. Whether or not a descendant or church owns individual plots and stones may also be unclear and may indeed vary according to state laws. Even within the realm of the law, the individual owner, once that owner has been established, may not have the right to do with a stone as he or she might please. The right, even, of municipalities to determine what is to be done with its stones may be overridden by the state's concern for preservation of its historical resources.

An old graveyard is a significant part of our cultural heritage, which, by that definition, belongs to us all and should be preserved for us all. Old gravestones, as objects of material culture, are important to society, and society is obliged to protect and preserve them, preferably in their original settings. Yet, there are occasions in which the only conscionable choice is for a museum to acquire one or several gravestones for their protection. In order that such acquisitions be effective and appropriate, criteria must be established to assist museums and interested individuals.

The decision to move a given stone indoors, a decision possibly involving individuals, museums, and government officials, must first consider urgency. Some cases are clear-cut, such as the approaching bulldozer preparing a building site, a river whose bed is moving into the graveyard, or even a dramatic increase in pollution, causing rapid stone deterioration. Other cases are much more difficult, and they may include gradually increasing vandalism in an area ill-equipped to deal with the problem, or a stone of particular significance that has recently received widespread attention. Yet even after that issue has been resolved, there remains the question of where the stone may be appropriately placed.

In most cases, simply removing a stone for storage elsewhere is not adequate. Storage too often becomes haphazard over the years and results in stones lying nearly forgotten and unidentifiable in basement corners, while dampness, fungi, and careless handling complete the deterioration process.

Almost the only appropriate caretaker is a recognized museum with the facilities and willingness to accept such an acquisition. In a few cases a church or government building might serve as a museum if it can properly display and care for the stone. Ideally, though, an artifact of importance should not be considered for removal unless a museum has agreed to accept it, to move it, to catalog it, and to make it as available for study and display as the other objects in its collections. Even if these criteria are met, however, the stone may not be as available as one might wish and certainly would not be as available as it is in the graveyard. Moreover, the scholar who wants to inspect both the original stone and its original setting must visit both the graveyard and the museum.

Finding a museum to take a particular stone may not be simple. As valuable as a particular old stone may be, a good museum must consider many factors before deciding to accept it. It will want to be sure, for example, that the marker is one whose period, decorative style, inscription, carver, and so on fit logically into the museum's collections and exhibition program; that its removal from the graveyard is not only legal but also acceptable to the museum's constituency; and that, set against other possible acquisitions, this artifact is important enough to occupy some of the always limited space in the museum's storage area. The additional problem with gravestone storage or exhibition is the extreme weight of many stones. To store one 500-pound stone may be feasible; to store ten may tax the capacity of some facilities.

The removal and transportation of these heavy, often fragile, artifacts are additional threats. Depending on its size and stability, moving a stone to another location may be a complex undertaking. Even after a facility has been found to receive it, the stone must be carefully removed from the ground, placed in a transfer box, and carried to the museum. The problems found in resetting stones are also evident here, in addition to the problems of transporting the stone some distance (figure 25).

Figure 25. Removal of a gravestone. Moving a stone is at best an unwieldy business; at worst, it can be dangerous. Here the Anthony Gwym gravestone (1776, Newburyport, Massachusetts) is being moved to the Boston Museum of Fine Arts. Photograph by Daniel Farber.

There is yet another consideration. When a stone has been removed, however appropriately, the act can have the unfortunate effect of encouraging a well-meaning individual, acting alone, to take another stone or stones indoors for safekeeping. Such action is never to be condoned. The act is theft and should be treated as such. Even descendants and churches cannot act independently of legal and ethical restrictions with regard to moving stones.

An issue not so clear-cut as theft concerns replacing a missing stone with a replica. Once a stone has been removed from the graveyard, some marker should remain in the yard indicating where the stone can be found. Excellent replications can be made, and poor ones, too, of course, but in all cases a replica comes up short in the area of aesthetics when compared with its original. Some are cut with a good copy of an authentic design, but the material used may be different from the original, sometimes even alien to the period and local availability of the original stone. Most are sandblasted rather than handcarved. Many of the best replicas are made of a composite stone mix that is cast from molds taken from the original stones, but even these do not have the exact characteristics of the originals' texture and color and line definition. The knowledgeable viewer can identify a replica, usually at a glance, but the casual visitor who notes a difference tends to accept the replica simply as unusual. It is important, therefore, that a replica be identified as such and that it show the year it was erected and the location of the original, if its original exists. This information should be inscribed on the back of the replica (figure 26).

Perhaps it is just as well that even the best replicas cannot quite duplicate the character of the original markers. More perfect replicas could encourage

Figure 26. A replica. The original sandstone gravemarker for the Reverend Moses Noyes, 1729, stands in Old Lyme, Connecticut, beside the recently cut granite replica of the missing original for the Reverend's son, Moses Noyes, Esq., 1743. Photograph by Daniel Farber.

unscrupulous antique dealers and collectors to sell original stones as copies and copies as originals.

The ethics of placing a replica in an old graveyard depends largely upon the reason the original is not in place. It would be very wrong indeed (and very expensive) to deface an old yard by discarding its weathered old stones and replacing them with replicas. On the other hand, replacing a marker that is forever gone could be a service, if the replica is properly identified and provided there is adequate information available (such as a rubbing or a photograph) to make a good replica. Without this information, it would be better to place at the site a plaque giving whatever information about the original is available.

In one yard several stones were severely damaged by a car, some beyond repair. Using photographs and fragments of those that could not be repaired, replicas were made and placed in the yard. The only problem was that the replacements were not identified as replicas. The knowledgeable person can easily identify them, but for others, especially in years to come, this omission will cause confusion. Another difficulty with replacements is that their availability can encourage a group to view as irreparable a stone that could have been saved. Even stones that have ben replaced because of severe deterioration or fragmentation beyond repair should be saved, in adequate storage, whenever possible.

Removal of a gravestone from the graveyard can be a complex or a simple process, depending on state laws, on the attitude of the community and civic authorities, the availability of a suitable museum for housing, and finally, the availability of funding. Funding is needed not only to move the stone but to repair the stone if necessary; to replace the original with a replica, if that is desired; and to set the replica.

Existing laws should be updated to deal with these and other problems related to the care of graveyards and removal of stones from the yard. In many cases, there are laws on the books regarding desecration, but they are often overlooked or obsolete. Twenty or fifty years ago, little consideration was given to the historic and artistic value of these stones, so existing legislation rarely deals with such issues and rarely reflects the importance of early stones. Here is another area where public education may be necessary. As suggested earlier, several states have enacted laws recently that give greater consideration to some of these problems. A copy of recent Massachusetts graveyard legislation is included in appendix D as one example of current efforts to address this problem legally. It may be used as a model, or it may provide a starting point for states that want to deal appropriately with their own problems regarding graveyard legislation.

A.

Figure 27. Museum safekeeping. (A) This stone for John Hoyle, 1642, is the oldest dated gravestone in New England. In the nineteenth century, it was placed for safekeeping in the Rhode Island Historical Society, where it can be viewed today. The slate replica that replaced it in the graveyard has been demolished. (B) This fine stone depicting Adam and Eve in the Garden of Eden was found abandoned in a Halifax, Nova Scotia, parking lot. It is now on permanent display in the Nova Scotia Museum, Halifax. Photographs by Daniel Farber.

B.

Removal of a stone should be considered only when all other options have been explored. It is a last resort and a radical one. The removal of even one stone can, in effect, begin the act of dismantling the graveyard, one stone at a time. In most cases, one's responsibility is to retain the integrity of the graveyard by preserving all of its stones intact in their original settings.

There do exist, however, a number of situations in which removal of a gravestone of exceptional artistic or historic significance is appropriate. Once such a situation has been clearly identified, to ignore that responsibility could cheat future generations of the opportunity to see and study these early American records and artifacts in the original (figure 27).

APPENDIX A
Sample Gravestone Rubbing Regulations

Permit for Headstone Rubbings

Permission is hereby given to _____

Representing _____

to do headstone rubbings according to the regulations of Milton

Cemetery on _____

Dated: _____

Superintendent: _____

Regulations for Headstone Rubbings

1. Headstone rubbings will be limited to sound stones only. Any stones that are cracked, split, spalling, flaking or have seams may not be rubbed.

2. Cleaning shall be limited to dusting with a soft brush. NO WIRE BRUSHES. *Do not* attempt to remove lichens or moss that may be growing on the stones.

3. The *entire* face of the stone shall be covered with paper held in place with masking tape.

4. *Do not* press hard when rubbing. Go over an area several times to darken it instead of pressing hard. Use short light strokes. Do small areas at a time.

5. *Do not* use inks, felt marking pens, or fiberglass tip marking pens.

6. All rubbings must be done under the direct supervision of a responsible adult.

7. The Milton Cemetery will not be held responsible for any injuries incurred.

8. All tape and paper must be removed from the stones and all rubbish will be disposed of and not left lying around.

9. It will be necessary to apply to the Superintendent at the Milton Cemetery Office for the permit each time rubbings are to be taken. Violation of any of the above regulations will void the permit and prevent acceptance of application for further permits by that individual or group.

MILTON CEMETERY
211 CENTRE STREET
MILTON, MASSACHUSETTS 02186

Phone 698-0200

JOHN E. CORWIN, *Superintendent*

To the Trustees of Milton Cemetery
211 Centre Street
Milton, Mass., 02186

Gentlemen:

I do hereby agree that I will accept full responsibility for any damage to headstones or the grounds incurred by me or the group under my supervision while engaged in taking headstone rubbings in Milton Cemetery on   19   , and I do hereby agree to follow the regulations for headstone rubbings presented to me with the permit.

_____

_____

Representing

_____

_____

Dated_____

APPENDIX B

Sample Cemetery Survey Forms

MASTER SURVEY CARD — 4

MATERIAL of which markers are made.   Approximate number of markers of each material:

_____ slate; _____ marble; _____ schist; _____ granite; _____ sandstone; _____ fieldstone;

other(s) _____

DECORATIVE CARVING on the markers.   Approximate number of stones with these motifs:

_____ skulls; _____ faces; _____ urns and/or willows; _____ other(s)

NAMES OF STONECARVERS whose work is in the cemetery, when known:

HISTORICAL BACKGROUND of the cemetery, if known.   For examples: Is the cemetery in its original location or moved? Are the markers in their original locations or rearranged? Has the cemetery been documented before, and if so, when? Are there unusual features or historical incidents which are of interest?

- -

FOLD ON DOTTED LINE

MASTER SURVEY CARD — 1

Name of cemetery _____   Master Card Number _____

Religious affiliations, if any _____   Year of cemetery survey _____

Person or group in charge _____   Recorder _____

LOCATION

_____
Nearest street/road/junction

_____
Nearest city/town   County   State

U.S.C.G.S. coordinates

Access *into* the cemetery: (check)
☐ by foot   ☐ by car

Orientation: Most stones face
☐ north ☐ south ☐ east ☐ west

Terrain: (check)
  ☐ level
  ☐ hilly—moderate
  ☐ hilly—steep

Bounded by:
  ☐ fence   ☐ hedge
  ☐ wall   ☐ other

Lighting:
  ☐ mostly shaded
  ☐ mostly unshaded

97

MASTER SURVEY CARD — 2

SIZE: Approximate number of markers
(check)

☐ over 2000   ☐ 1000
☐ 2000   ☐ 500
☐ 1750   ☐ 250
☐ 1500   ☐ 100
☐ 1250   ☐ fewer than 100

Approximate area size

_____ ft. x _____ ft.
or
_____ meters x _____ meters

AGE: _____ earliest date

_____ most recent date

Approximate number of markers w/dates from:

_____ 17th century   _____ 19th century

_____ 18th century   _____ 20th century

CONDITION OF THE GROUNDS

Overall Evaluation
(check)

☐ generally excellent
☐ generally good
☐ generally fair
☐ generally poor

Specific Problems
(check)

☐ overgrown vines
☐ overgrown grass
☐ overgrown shrubs
☐ unpruned trees
☐ fences, walls in poor repair

☐ other(s)

- -

MASTER SURVEY CARD — 3

CONDITION OF THE MARKERS

Overall Evaluation
(check)

☐ generally excellent
☐ generally good
☐ generally fair
☐ generally poor

Specific Problems
(give number)

_____ badly tilted stones
_____ fragments on ground
_____ broken but standing
_____ damaged surfaces

Restorations
(give number)

_____ metal supports
_____ capped w/metal
_____ set in concrete
_____ enclosed in concrete
_____ repaired w/adhesive
_____ painted to protect
_____. other_____

Footstones
(check)

☐ none, or very few
☐ reset behind headstones
☐ in original positions

NORTH CAROLINA CEMETERY SURVEY

1. Location

   a) Name or names of cemetery _____

   b) Country_____

   c) City, town, community, or township _____

   d) Specific location _____

   e) Property owned by _____

   f) U.S.G.S. Topographic Map: Quadrangle_____

     1) Cemetery coordinates: Latitude _____ Longitude _____

     2) Cemetery number on map

2. Classification

   a) Public: ☐ Municipal ☐County ☐State ☐Federal

   b) Private: ☐ Family ☐ Church (denomination _____) ☐ Fraternal

   ☐ Other, explain _____

   c) Status: ☐ Abandoned ☐ Maintained, but not used ☐ Currently being used

   d) Size: Approximate number of graves _____ Approximate size of cemetery __

   e) Type: ☐ American Indian ☐ Black ☐ Slave ☐White

   ☐ Other, explain _____

3. Accessibility to Public

   a) ☐ Unrestricted b)☐ Restricted, explain _____

4. Condition

   a) ☐ Well maintained and preserved   b)☐ Poorly maintained

   c) ☐ Overgrown, easily identifiable   d)☐ Overgrown, not easily identifiable

   e) ☐ Not identifiable as a burial site, but known to exist through tradition or other means. Explain _____

5. Cemetery Enclosure

   a) Is the cemetery enclosed by a wall, fence, hedge, etc.? ☐

   If yes, specify how it is enclosed _____

   b) State condition of wall, fence, hedge, etc. _____

6. Tombstones or Markers

    a) Are stones or markers present? ☐   b) If yes, are they inscribed? ☐

    c) Number of readable stones or markers ☐   d) Date of last know burial ☐

    e) Date of earliest known burial ☐   f) Are there unusual stones? ☐

    Describe them. _____

    _____

    g) Have markers been damaged? ☐ If yes, by farm animals? ☐ Vandalism?
    ☐ Farming operations? ☐ Industrial operations? ☐ Custodial care? ☐ Other
    means? Explain _____

7. Note any hazards imperiling the cemetery's existence _____

    _____

8. Has this cemetery been listed in an existing published or unpublished cemetery survey? ☐ If yes, explain _____

9. Historical or other special significance of cemetery, if any _____

    _____

    _____

10. Any other information _____

    _____

    _____

    Canvasser _____

    Date _____

    Organization _____

    Address _____

This form has been prepared for use by the Committee for the Study of Abandoned Cemeteries, a group created in 1978 by the North Carolina General Assembly to study the number, nature, and condition of North Carolina's cemeteries. Inquiries concerning the study should be addressed to Cemetery Survey, North Carolina Division of Archives and History, 109 East Jones Street, Raleigh, North Carolina 27611.

CEMETERY SURVEY
INDIVIDUAL MARKER RECORD CARD

14 13 12 11 10 9 8 7 6 5 4 3 2 1

Cemetery or Graveyard _____

Religious Affiliation (if any) _____

1. Master Record Number _____
2. Date of Record _____
3. Name of Recorder or Group _____
4. Marker Number (from Grid) _____
5. Marker Type: 1. Table   2. Head   3. Foot   4. Tomb   5. Family   6. Other _____
6. Material: 1. Slate   2. Marble   3. Granite   4. Sandstone   5. Schist   6. Fieldstone _____
7. Stonecarver _____
8. How many surfaces are carved? _____
9. Carving technique used: 1. Incised   2. Relief   3. High   4. Three dimensional _____
10. Decorative carving motif(s):   1. Skull   2. Face   3. Urn and/or willow
    4. Lettering only   5. Other(s) _____
11. Number of people commemorated _____
12. Condition of marker: 1. Sound   2. Unsound—chipped   3. Unsound—cracked
    4. Unsound—Crumbled   5. Eroded   6. Broken   7. Tilted   8. Sunken   9. Discolored/Stained
    10. Moss/Lichen covered   11. Overgrown (vines, grass, brush)
    12. Repaired or protected   13. In situ   14. Displaced _____
13. Condition of the inscription: 1. Mint   2. Clear but worn   3. Mostly decipherable
    4. Traces   5. Illegible or destroyed _____
14. Dimensions (in centimeters)   Height_____ Width_____ Thickness_____
15. Photograph negative number _____
16. Which way marker faces? (circle)

   N   S   E   W   NE   SE   NW   SW

PHOTOGRAPH	INSCRIPTION
REMARKS	

Survey card for individual markers.

St. Paul Cemetery INVENTORY OF MARKERS

Date of record _____

Cataloguer _____

Marker # (from grid)_____

Photo Negative # _____

Marker type: 1. Head 2. Foot 3. Table 4. Tomb 5. Other _____

Material: 1. Slate 2. Slate with pyrites 3. Sandstone 4. Marble 5. Sandstone with marble insert 6. Granite 7. Other _____

Tomb Supports: 1. Stone and mortar 2. Brick 3. Panel 4. Not visible

Carved Surfaces: 1. Front 2. Back 3. Top 4. Side panels 5. End panels

Carving motif: 1. Winged skull 2. Winged head 3. Urn 4. Urn & willow 5. Lettering only 6. Hourglass 7. Rosette(s) 8. Border 9. Other _____

Condition of marker: 1. Sound 2. Chipped 3. Cracked 4. Crumbled

_____ 5. Eroded 6. Broken 7. Tilted 8. Sunken

_____ 9. Insert missing 10. Panel fallen/broken, missing

_____ 11. Discolored/stained 12. Moss/lichen 13. Other*

Condition of the inscription: 1. Mint 2. Clear but worn 3. Mostly decipherable 4. Traces 5. Illegible or destroyed 6. Underground

Dimensions: (in centimetres) Height   Width   Thickness

Direction marker faces: N S E W NE SE NW SW

	Subject Cross-Reference
Inscription _____	
_____	
_____	
_____	

Epitaph: _____

_____

Cataloguer's remarks:_____

APPENDIX C
Consultants, Contractors, Conservators, and Carvers

The following are consultants, information specialists, or stonework practitioners who may be able to provide information directly or refer you to sources in your area.

American Building Restoration Co., Frank Genello, 18 White Street, Newport, Rhode Island 02840; (401) 849-3941.

Restoration contractor.

Barre Granite Association, P.O. Box 481, Barre, Vermont 05641; (802) 476-4131.

Represents many modern monument makers and suppliers of granite and materials for its care. Available for advice concerning modern monument care.

F.B. Bunyard, 791 Tremont Street, Box W-111, Boston, Massachusetts 02118; (617) 536-1961.

Sculptor and letter-carver, working primarily in slate. May consider some restoration and repair.

Center for Conservation and Technical Studies, Harvard University Art Museums, 32 Quincy Street, Cambridge, Massachusetts 02138; (617) 495-2392.

Objects conservators working primarily with museum objects but will consider consulting on gravestone work.

Center for Preservation Research, 400 Avery Hall, Columbia University, New York, New York 10027; (212) 280-3973 or (212) 280-8712.

Conservators providing technical information, condition analysis, and restoration services.

Dennis and Craine, 17 Tudor Street, Cambridge, Massachusetts 02139; (617) 497-4027.

Objects conservators specializing in monument conservation, particularly bronze and stone.

Lance Mayer, c/o Lyman Allyn Museum, 625 Williams Street, New London, Connecticut 06320; (203) 443-2618.

Conservator with experience in graveyard preservation.

Peter McCarthy, Almont Memorials, 201 Santa Fe Drive, Pueblo, Colorado 81006; (303) 561-1033.

Modern monument maker. Familiar with the problems of historical restoration.

Casimer Michalczyk, 2095 Main Street, Glastonbury, Connecticut 06033; (203) 633-7163 (winter); 28 Siloam Avenue, P.O. Box 335, Oak Bluffs, Massachusetts 02557; (617) 693-3108 (summer).

Sculptor and carver of slate gravestones. Will consider restoration stonework and consulting.

A. Monti Granite Company, Inc., 266 Centre Street, Quincy, Massachusetts 02169; (617) 471-8989.

Suppliers of granite, marble, and slate. Repairs stone.

Preservation Technology Associates, Inc., 101 Tremont Street, Boston, Massachusetts 02108; (617) 423-3780.

Consultants in masonry restoration, repair, conservation, and replacement.

Society for the Preservation of New England Antiquities (SPNEA), Conservation Center, Lyman Estate, 185 Lyman Street, Waltham, Massachusetts 02154; (617) 891-1985.

Excellent source for qualified personnel in the New England area.

State Historic Preservation Officer in your state.

To locate this individual, check with your state historical society or state department of history.

The John Stevens Shop, John Benson, 29 Thames Street, Newport, Rhode Island 02840; (401) 846-0566.

Famous for hand-carved lettering and relief carving.

Lynette Strangstad, Stone Faces, P.O. Box 21090, Charleston, South Carolina 29413-1090; (803) 762-6025.

Services in graveyard preservation planning; graveyard preservation workshops; gravemarker conservation; architectural stone restoration.

While the procedures outlined in this manual are accepted practices in the field of stone conservation, and while the above are reputable individuals and firms within their fields, neither the Association for Gravestone Studies nor the author nor the publisher assumes any responsibility for the preservation, conservation, consulting, or restoration work of readers of this publication or for the work of those listed here.

APPENDIX D
Sample Cemetery Legislation

Massachusetts Laws Relating to Gravestone Preservation

General Laws, Chapter 114

16. Appropriation for and Care of Certain Cemeteries. Any town may annually appropriate and raise by taxation such sums as may be necessary to care for and keep in good order and to protect by proper fences any or all burial grounds within the town in which ten or more bodies are interred and which are not properly cared for by the owners, and the care and protection of such burial grounds shall be in charge of the cemetery commissioners, if the town has such officers, otherwise in charge of its selectmen.

17. Ancient Burial Places to Be Preserved. A town shall not alienate or appropriate to any other use than that of a burial ground any tract of land which has been for more than one hundred years used as a burial place; and no portion of such burial ground shall be taken for public use without special authority from the general court. "Burial place," as referred to in this section, shall include unmarked burial grounds known or suspected to contain the remains of one or more American Indians.

18. Care of Neglected Burial Places. Any town having within its limits an abandoned or neglected burying ground may take charge of the same and keep it in good order, and may appropriate money therefore, but no property rights shall be violated and no body shall be disinterred. No fence, tomb, monument, or other structure shall be removed or destroyed, but the same may be repaired or restored.

Chapter 272

71. Unlawful Disinterment. Whoever, not being lawfully authorized by the proper authorities, willfully digs up, disinters, removes, or conveys away a human body, or the remains thereof, or knowingly aids in such disinterment, removal, or conveying away, and whoever is accessory thereto either

before or after the fact, shall be punished by imprisonment in the state prison for not more than three years or in jail for not more than two and one-half years or by a fine of not more than four thousand dollars.

73. Whoever willfully destroys, mutilates, defaces, injures, or removes a tomb, monument, gravestone, veteran's gravemarker or metal plaque or flag, or other structure or thing which is placed or designed for a memorial of the dead, or a fence railing, curb, or other thing which is intended for the protection or ornament of a structure or thing before mentioned or of an enclosure for the burial of the dead, or willfully removes, destroys, mutilates, cuts, breaks or injures a tree, shrub, or plant placed or being within such enclosure, or wantonly or maliciously disturbs the contents of a tomb or a grave, shall be punished by imprisonment in the state prison for not more than five years or by imprisonment in the jail or house of correction for not more than two and one-half years and by a fine of not more than five thousand dollars.

73A. (Added by Chapter 448 of the Acts of 1973) Removal of Gravestones and Other Memorials for the Purpose of Repair or Reproduction. In any city or town which accepts this section, the provisions of Section 73 shall not prohibit the removal, in accordance with rules and regulations promulgated by the state secretary, of a gravestone or other structure or thing which is placed or designed as a memorial for the dead, for the purpose of repair or reproduction thereof by community sponsored, educationally oriented, and professionally directed repair teams.

75. Removal of Flowers, Flags, or Memorial Tokens. Whoever, without authority, removes flowers, flags, or memorial tokens from any grave, tomb, monument, or burial lot in any cemetery or other place of burial shall be punished by a fine of not more than five thousand dollars or by imprisonment for not more than six months.

Rules and Regulations Issued by the Secretary of State

1. Permits to restore and reproduce gravestones under the provisions of Chapter 448 of the Acts of 1973 shall be issued by the Secretary of the Commonwealth after he shall have satisfied himself that the proposals for such restoration and/or reproduction meet the standards of educational value, community interest, and professional competence. In making this determination, the Secretary may call upon the assistance of the staff and members of the Massachusetts Historical Commission, local historical district commissions, and local, regional, statewide and national historical and other learned societies and individuals whose experience he may deem relevant.

2. Reproduction of the gravestones may only be done for historical purposes by nonprofit organizations.

3. Request for a permit must be submitted upon application form and shall give a detailed plan of the gravestone restoration project.

GLOSSARY

ARTIFICIAL STONE. A term used to describe various materials also known as *art marble, artificial marble, cast stone,* and *composite stone.* Some mixture of stone chips or fragments is generally embedded in a matrix of cement or plaster, and the surface may be ground, polished, molded, or otherwise treated to simulate stone.

BLUESTONE. A trade term applied to hard, fine-grained, commonly feldspathic and micaceous sandstone or siltstone of dark greenish to bluish gray color that splits readily along bedding planes to form thin slabs. Commonly used to pave surfaces for pedestrian traffic, this material may occasionally be seen in gravestones.

BOXTOMB. A grave monument resembling a box, usually about 3' X 6' and 2' to 3' high, making an individual grave, or occasionally a family or other multiple burial. Such structures may be known locally as crypts; burial, however, is generally below ground with construction taking place following burial.

BROWNSTONE. A trade term applied to ferruginous dark brown and reddish brown sandstone quarried and extensively used for building in the eastern United States during the middle and late nineteenth century. Most later use has been for renovation, repair, or additions to structures in which the stone was originally used. In gravestones, most commonly used as bases, although common in some areas, such as the Connecticut River Valley, for tabletstones as well.

CALCITE. A mineral form of calcium carbonate. Principal constituent of most limestones.

COMPOSITE STONE. See ARTIFICIAL STONE.

DELAMINATION. Separation of layers of stone along bedding planes.

DOLOMITE. 1. Mineral form of calcium-magnesium carbonate. Constituent of some building limestone. 2. Limestone consisting principally of the mineral dolomite.

DOLOMITIC LIMESTONE. Limestone that contains more than 10 percent but less than 80 percent of the mineral dolomite.

EFFLORESCENCE. On masonry, a film or encrustation of soluble salts, generally white and most commonly consisting of calcium sulfate, that may deposit on the surface of stone, brick, or mortar if moisture moves through the masonry. Often caused by free alkalies leached from mortar or adjacent concrete.

EXFOLIATION. Peeling or scaling of stone surfaces caused by chemical or physical weathering.

FACE. In stone masonry, the surface visible after setting. In gravestones, commonly the carved surface of tabletstones and slabs.

FLAKING. A term commonly used regarding gravestones to indicate minor delamination of surfaces or otherwise unsound stone which easily peels off in small sheets or layers.

FOOTSTONE. In the seventeenth and eighteenth century, a grave was generally marked by both a stone at the head and a stone at the foot. Footstones are smaller and more simply inscribed than their headstones. If they bear any carving, it is usually only the name or initials of the deceased, perhaps the death date, and sometimes a simple decorative design.

GNEISS. Coarse-grained metamorphic rock with discontinuous foliation. When used for building stone, generally classed as trade granite. Most gneisses are dark and composed mainly of quartz, feldspar, mica, and ferromagnesian minerals (iron-magnesium silicates).

GRANITE. Geologically, igneous rock with crystals or grains of visible size and consisting mainly of quartz and the sodium or potassium feldspars. In building stone and gravestones, crystalline silicate rock with visible grains. The commercial term includes gneiss and igneous rocks that are not granite in the strictest sense.

IGNEOUS ROCKS. Rock formed by change of the molten material called magma to the solid state. The igneous rocks are one of three generic classes of rocks (igneous, sedimentary, and metamorphic). Various igneous rocks, generally termed granite if coarse grained, are used for building stone and gravestones.

INCISED CARVING. In gravestones, ornamentation made by cutting into the stone; engraving.

LAMINATED STONE. Stone consisting of thin sheets; stone built up in layers, such as slate.

LIMESTONE. Rock of sedimentary origin composed principally of calcite or dolomite or both. Commonly used in gravestones and tomb structures, in some cases considered to be marble.

MARBLE. Geologically, a metamorphic rock made up largely of calcite or dolomite. As used commercially, the term includes many dense limestones and some rock dolomites. Numerous minerals may be present in minor to significant amounts in marble, and their presence and distribution account for much of the distinctive appearance that many marbles possess. The predominant stone for gravestones in the nineteenth century.

METAMORPHIC ROCK. Rock altered in appearance, density, and crystalline structure, and in some cases mineral composition, by high temperature or high pressure or both. Slate is derived from shale, quartzite from quartz sandstone, and true marble from limestone.

MICA. A group of silicate minerals characterized by nearly perfect basal cleavage, causing them to split readily into extremely thin plates. The micas are prominent constituents of metamorphic and igneous rocks. In gravestones, they are often apparent in brownstones.

PATCH. Compound used to fill natural voids or to replace chips and broken corners or edges in fabricated pieces of cut stone. Applied in plastic form. Mixed or selected to match the stone in color and texture.

RELIEF CARVING. Ornamentation projecting forward from a surface through shallow or, occasionally in gravestones, deep carving.

RISING DAMP. Moisture carried upward through porous stone by capillary action. Soluble salts in the ground beneath a gravestone may be introduced into a stone through this process. If the salts crystallize within the pores of the stone, the action may cause the surface to break off, known as spalling; if the salts are carried to the surface of the stone and then crystallize on it, efflorescence is formed.

SANDSTONE. Sedimentary rock composed of sand-sized grains naturally cemented by mineral material. In most sandstone used for building and gravestones, quartz grains predominate.

SCHIST. Metamorphic rock with continuous foliation. Splits along foliation and is occasionally found in gravestone use.

SEDIMENTARY ROCK. Rock formed from materials deposited as sediments, in the sea, in fresh water, or on the land. The materials are transported to their site of deposition by such forces as running water, wind, or moving ice. They may deposit as fragments or by precipitation from solution. Limestone and sandstone are the sedimentary rocks most used for building and gravestones.

SHALE. A rock of clay origin, easily split into layers. Occasionally found in gravestones.

SLATE. A hard, brittle metamorphic rock consisting mainly of clay minerals and characterized by good cleavage that is unrelated to the bedding in the earlier shale or clay from which it formed. A popular gravestone material of the eighteenth century, particularly in coastal areas. Many of the best-preserved examples of gravestone art are found in slate, an extremely stable stone.

SOAPSTONE. Massive soft rock that contains a high proportion of talc. Occasionally used in gravestones.

SPALL. In stone, to flake or split away through frost action or pressure. As a noun, a chip or flake of stone.

TABLE STONE or TABLE TOMB. A type of grave monument in which a stone slab, usually at least two inches thick by about three feet wide by six feet long, is supported by six pillars or columns. The columns, or legs, usually from two to three feet high, in turn rest on a stone set at ground level. The structure covers the gravesite, giving the appearance of a stone table. In most cases, an inscription is written on the slab top; the stone columns are generally carved, sometimes ornately.

TABLETSTONE. A stone gravemarker consisting of a single piece of stone usually not more than three inches thick and set vertically in the ground; to be distinguished from a table stone or vault.

TYMPANUM. In gravestones, the semicircular (or occasionally triangular) decorated face at the top of a tabletstone.

SOURCES OF ADDITIONAL INFORMATION

Two sources for a variety of gravestone-related publications are:

Association for Gravestone Studies, 30 Elm Street, Worcester, Massachusetts 01609, and Center for Thanatology Research, 391 Atlantic Avenue, Brooklyn, New York 11217.

Some of the publications listed below recommend procedures that are not approved by professionals and conflict with recommendations presented in this book. You will do well to follow this book's carefully considered recommendations. Despite their occasional differences of opinion and judgment, all the publications listed will provide worthwhile background information about graveyard preservation.

Archaeology

Archaeology and Preservation, Rex Wilson. Information Sheet no. 28. Washington D.C.: National Trust for Historic Preservation, 1980. 20 pages.

A brochure describing the nature and importance of archaeology. Useful in understanding archaeology as it relates to graveyards.

Art in Gravestone Carving

Early American Gravestone Art in Photographs, Francis Y. Duval and Ivan B. Rigby. New York: Dover Publications, 1978. 133 pages.

A selection of 200 examples of exceptional gravestone art. Excellent reproduction of photographs and documentation.

Early Gravestone Art in Georgia and South Carolina, Diana Williams Combs. Athens, Ga.: University of Georgia Press, 1986. 246 pages.

Examination of gravestone iconography, symbolism, and carvers in Georgia and South Carolina, especially coastal areas. Photographs.

Folk Art in Stone, Southwest, Virginia, Klaus Wust. Edinburg, Va.: Shenan-
doah History, 1970. 28 pages.

A booklet describing graveyards, stonecutters, and motifs common to
the southwest Virginia landscape.

A Grave Business: New England Gravestone Rubbings, A Selection, Susan
Kelly and Anne Williams. New Haven, Conn.: S.Z. Field Co., Art
Resources of Connecticut, 1979. 42 pages.

Published with a traveling exhibition of Kelly and Williams's rubbings.
Includes catalog of rubbings in the exhibition with notations about the
work exhibited and the stonecarver. Includes a sound and succinct
introduction to early gravestone art.

Graven Images, Allan L. Ludwig. Middletown, Conn.: Wesleyan University
Press, 1966. 482 pages.

A book of New England stonecarvings and the area's symbols, explor-
ing Puritan theology, religious history, folklore, and anthropology. Well
illustrated and considered a classic in its field.

*Gravestone Designs — Rubbings and Photographs from Early New York and
New Jersey,* Emily Wasserman. New York: Dover Publications, 1972. 190
pages.

Short text introduces early carving styles of the two states. Photographs
and rubbings make up the bulk of the volume. 220 illustrations.

Gravestones of Early New England and the Men Who Made Them, 1653-1800,
Harriette Merrifield Forbes. Boston: Houghton Mifflin, 1927. Reprint,
Princeton: Pyne Press, 1955. 141 pages.

The first book focusing on New England's seventeenth- and eighteenth-
century gravestones as art objects and their carvers as sculptors. The first
attributions of work to named carvers and first research into their lives
and carving styles. Photographs, index. All editions now out of print
but available in libraries.

*Masks of Orthodoxy: Folk Gravestone Carving in Plymouth County, Mas-
sachusetts, 1689-1805,* Peter Benes. Amherst: University of Massachusetts
Press, 1977. 273 pages.

Detailed study of Puritan gravestone art and symbolism of the area and
period. Research on carver attributions. Profusely illustrated with photographs and line drawings. Bibliography, index.

Memento Mori: The Gravestones of Early Long Island, 1680-1810, Richard
F. Welch. Syosset, N.Y.: Friends of Long Island's Heritage, 1983. 94 pages.

Introduction to early Long Island graveyards, their historical background,
carving styles, and important stones and carvers of the area. List of Long
Island yards and carvers represented in each. Photographs.

*Memorials for Children of Change—The Art of Early New England Stone-
carving,* Dickran and Ann Tashjian. Middletown, Conn.: Wesleyan University Press, 1974. 309 pages.

Historical background, iconographic sources, symbolism of seventeenth-
and eighteenth-century gravestone art in New England. Full epitaphs
of illustrated stones. Well illustrated with photographs and rubbings.
The quality of the rubbings is outstanding.

Documentation

"Cemetery Transcribing: Preparations and Procedures," American Association for State and Local History Technical Leaflet 9, *History News* 26
(May 1971). 12 pages.

A discussion of techniques used in reading and recording gravestones,
including how to find "lost" cemeteries, tools needed, how to read difficult stones, mapping, and sample transcription record of small graveyard.

How to Record Graveyards, Jeremy Jones. London: Council for British
Archaeology; and Hertford: Trust for British Archaeology (RESCUE), 1976.
40 pages.

Why and how to record, map, and photograph gravestones and graveyards.

"Photographing Tombstones: Equipment and Techniques," Mary Ellen Jones.
American Association for State and Local History Technical Leaflet 92,
History News 32 (February 1977). 8 pages.

Provides information regarding the importance of photographing gravestones, useful equipment and techniques, and documentation and
fieldwork.

"Recording Cemetery Data," J. Joanna Baker, Daniel Farber, and Anne G.
Giesecke. *Markers: The Journal of the Association for Gravestone Studies*
1 (1980). 20 pages.

An excellent article on recording gravestone inscriptions, mapping a cemetery, and photographing gravestones.

Education and Public Awareness

A Cemetery Survey—Teacher's Manual, Betty Ann Mulligan and Deborah Trask. Halifax, Nova Scotia: Nova Scotia Museum, 1974.

Suggestions for teachers taking classes to graveyards to study local history. Includes notes for prior class preparation, suggestions for data to gather, and questions following field trip. Designed to accompany a multimedia school loan kit, which includes stone samples, data sheets, *Life How Short, Eternity How Long,* "Folk Art in Stone," cemetery survey suggestions, and more.

Journal from the Gloucester Experiment, Alfred M. Duca. Annisquam, Mass.: New England Program for Teacher Education, 1974. 86 pages.

Description of a school community project.

Epitaphs

American Epitaphs, Grave and Humorous, Charles L. Wallis. New York: Dover Publications, 1973.

Epitaphs and Icons, Cape Cod, Martha's Vineyard, Diana Hume George and A. Nelson. Orleans, Mass.: Parnassus Imprints, 1983, 128 pages.

Granite Laughter and Marble Tears, Robert E. Pike. Brattleboro, Vt.: Stephen Daye Press, 1938. 80 pages.

Stranger, Stop and Cast an Eye: A Guide to Gravestones and Gravestone Rubbing, G. W. Jacobs. Brattleboto, Vt., Stephene Greene Press, 1973. 123 pages.

Contains section on history of grave symbols and stonecutters, followed by a section on five rubbing techniques. Good step-by-step descriptions. Well illustrated.

Funding

Foundation Center, 888 7th Avenue, New York, New York 10019.

Offers information and advice to grant seekers.

Foundation Grants Index. New York: Foundation Center, fifteenth edition, 1986.

Lists grant sources. Available at libraries.

Grantsmanship Center, 1031 South Grand Avenue, Los Angeles, California 90015.

Offers a variety of publications related to grant seeking, including the Grantsmanship Library; offers seminars valuable to grant seekers.

General

"Conservation/Preservation," *The AGS Newsletter* 7:4 (Fall 1983), part 2. 6 pages.

A potpourri of ideas and suggestions for preservation, plus accounts of experiences of laymen.

The AGS Series of Regional Guides to 17th- and 18th-Century Graveyards, Francis Duval, editor. Needham, Mass.: AGS Publications, n.d.

A series in preparation, with two guides now available: Guide 1: *Narragansett Bay Area Graveyards* (eastern Rhode Island and parts of southern Massachusetts), Vincent Luti (no date), 17 pages. Guide 2: *Long Island, New York, Graveyards (including Lower Manhattan Island,* Richard Welch (1986), 16 pages.

"Cemetery Art Fights for Life," Elizabeth Morse and Edwin Connelly. *Historic Preservation,* July/August 1981. Available in reprint (6 pages) from the Center for Thanatology Research, 391 Atlantic Avenue, Brooklyn, New York 11217.

An article stating the need for and importance of graveyard preservation measures.

Epitaph and Icon: Field Guide to the Old Burying Grounds of Cape Cod, Martha's Vineyard, and Nantucket, Diana Hume George and Malcolm A. Nelson. Orleans, Mass.: Parnassus Imprints, 1983. 128 pages.

Introduction to eighteenth-century graveyards, gravestones, and historical background, along with field guide to area yards. Notes on gravestone photography, stone rubbing, and data collection. Photographs.

Life How Short, Eternity How Long: Gravestone Carving and Carvers in Nova Scotia, Deborah Trask. Halifax, Nova Scotia: Nova Scotia Museum, 1978. 142 pages.

Historical background and description of dominant eighteenth- and nineteenth-century carving styles of local and imported stones. Research on carver attribution. List of carvers and marble works in Nova Scotia. Bibliography. Illustrations.

Markers: The Journal of the Association for Gravestone Studies, vol. 1, 1979/80. 128 pages.

Fifteen articles relating to gravestone and graveyard preservation and other gravestone-related topics. See especially, "Recording Cemetery Data," by F. Joanne Baker, Daniel Farber, and Anne G. Giesecke; "The Care of Old Cemeteries and Gravestones," by Lance Mayer; and "Protective Custody," by Robert Emlen. Illustrated.

"A Neglected Legacy," and "While There Is Still Time," Francis Duval and Ivan Rigby. *Ohio Antique Review,* April and May 1982. (Available in reprint, 6 pages, from the Center for Thanatology Research, 391 Atlantic Avenue, Brooklyn, New York 11217.)

Written for the layman with the assistance of a conservator.

New England Cemeteries: A Collector's Guide, Andrew Kull. Brattleboro, VT.; Stephen Greene Press, 1975. 253 pages.

Good directions for finding 262 interesting New England cemeteries. Symbols used to indicate "unusually picturesque" cemeteries, "interesting carving," "famous people," and/or a "grand style."

Preserving Historical Cemeteries, Sherene Baugher, Gina Santucci, Robert W. Venables, and Gaynell Stone. New York: New York City Landmarks Preservation Commission, n.d. 4 pages.

An introductory brochure emphasizing the importance of markers, threats to them, and basic viewpoint toward their preservation. Useful in preparing your own brochure.

Protecting and Preserving Old Burial Grounds, James W. Bradley. Boston: Massachusetts Historical Commission, n.d. 3 pages.

Different in format but similar in content to the New York City brochure, above.

Stones: 18th-Century Scottish Gravestones, Betty Willsher and Doreen Hunter. New York: Taplinger Publishing Company, 1979. 139 pages.

Description of the carving and symbolism of Scotland's most important eighteenth-century gravestone sculpture. A comprehensive guide. List of Adam and Eve stones. List of Scottish yard. Photographs.

Tales of the Old Dutch Graveyard: A Walking Tour. Tarrytown, N.Y.: Heritage Committee, Junior League of Westchester-on-Hudson, n.d.

A useful model for graveyard walking tours.

With Bodilie Eyes: Eschatological Themes in Puritan Literature and Grave-stone Art, David Watters. Ann Arbor: UMI Research Press, 1981. 247 pages.

A scholarly examination of Puritan beliefs regarding death and afterlife as seen in Puritan literature and gravestone art.

Gravestone Rubbing

Oldstone's Guide to Creative Rubbing, Glen K. Marks. Boston: Oldstone Enterprises, 1973. 21 pages.

Introduces gravestones, monumental brasses, historical markers, and collages as subjects for wax rubbings. Illustrated.

Reproducing Relief Surfaces: A Complete Handbook of Rubbing, Dabbing, Casting, and Daubing, William J. A. McGeer. 1972. 40 pages. (Available from the author, 48 Harwood Avenue, Littleton, Massachusetts 01460.)

Rubbing for Beginners, Jessie Lie Farber. Needham, Mass.; AGS Publications, n.d. 2 pages.

How to make a rubbing, with emphasis on the responsibility of the rubber for the care of the stone.

Rubbings and Textures: A Graphic Technique, John J. Bodor. New York: Reinhold Book Corporation, 1968. 107 pages.

Excellent and thorough description of five techniques for rubbing a variety of subjects. A separate chapter on New England gravestones as rubbing subjects, and a chapter each on the historical background of rubbing, suggestions for teachers, and suggestions for cataloging, storing, displaying, and photographing rubbings.

New York Is a Rubber's Paradise, Roberta Halporn. 1980. 11 pages. (Available from Highly Specialized Promotions, 391 Atlantic Avenue, Brooklyn, New York 11217.)

Landscaping

The Victorian Celebration of Death: The Architecture and Planning of 19th-Century Necropolis, James S. Curl. London: Constable and Co.; and New York: Charles Scribners' Sons, 1980. 222 pages.

Legal Considerations

An Act for the Preservation and Care of Burial Places and Memorials for the Dead, Theodore Chase. Needham, Mass.: AGS Publications, n.d. 1 page.

A model to assist civic groups in lobbying for improved protective legislation.

Preservation and Conservation

"An Introduction to Repointing," by Robert C. Mack and James S. Askins, APT Bulletin, Vol. XI, No. 3, 1979. Association for Preservation Technology, P.O. Box 2487, Station D, Ohawa, Ontario, Canada K1P 5W6.

Good introduction to this restoration procedure. Other articles may also be of interest.

"The Care of Old Cemeteries and Gravestones," Lance Mayer. *Markers: The Journal of the Association for Gravestone Studies* 1 (1979/80). 12 pages. (Reprint available from AGS Publications, 46 Plymouth Road, Needham, Massachusetts 02192.

A careful, professional dicussion of graveyard and gravestone preservation problems and some solutions.

Cemetery Restoration and Preservation: Some Resources and Other Considerations, Jessie Lie Farber. Needham, Mass.: AGS Publications, n.d. 3 pages.

An introduction. Points laymen in the right direction.

The Churchyard's Handbook, 2nd edition, Henry Stapleton, F.S.A., and Peter Burman, F.S.A. London: CIO Publishing, 1976. 136 pages.

Advice on the care and maintenance of churchyards; designed for use in English yards, but contains much relevant general information.

The Cleaning and Waterproof Coating of Masonry Buildings, Robert C. Mack. Preservation Brief no.1. National Park Service, Technical Services Division. Washington, D.C.: Government Printing Office, 1975. 4 pages.

Recommended by the Massachusetts Historical Commission.

Discovering, Restoring, and Maintaining Old Cemeteries, Theodore Brown. Augusta, Me.: Maine Old Cemetery Association, n.d. 9 pages. (Also available from the Center for Thanatology Research, 391 Atlantic Avenue, Brooklyn, New York 11217.

For Maine Old Cemetery Association members and others working to save abandoned burial grounds.

Graveyard Restoration Hand Book, Carleton R. Vance. n.d. 24 pages. (Available from New Hampshire Old Graveyard Association, 445 Greeley Street, Manchester, New Hampshire 03102.

Ideas and instructions for the amateur.

"How to Clean and Polish Marble," Lynette Strangstad. *Old-House Journal* 10 (October 1982). 4 pages.

Describes poulticing procedures and lists appropriate solvents for removing various stains.

A Manual for Graveyard Conservation, Gordon Kinsman, Deborah Trask, Harry Nelson, and Leslie Blackburn. Truro, Nova Scotia: Colchester Historical Museum, 1979. 30 pages.

A practical approach to restoration addressed to local historical societies by a varied team of professionals.

Recommendations for the Care of Gravestones, Jessie Lie Farber. Needham, Mass.: AGS Publications, n.d. 2 pages.

Do's and don'ts for the layman. Brief, practical overview.

Repointing Mortar Joints in Historic Buildings, Robert C. Mack, A.I.A. Preservation Brief no. 2. Revised. National Park Service, Technical Services Division. Washington, D.C.: U.S. Government Printing Office, 1980. 7 pages.

Tells how to repoint mortar joints specifically and indicates brickwork specifications appropriate for historic structures. Applicable to tomb structures of brick construction.

The modern monument industry has developed some excellent guides to assist monument makers in the repair of modern cemetery monuments. This literature is not listed here because it is addressed to experienced members of the modern monument industry and can be misused by the layman. Also, the recommended procedures and techniques apply primarily to granite repair and would not necessarily be appropriate for the repair of ancient sandstone, slate, and marble.

INDEX

Acid rain, 60, 86

Acids, 48, 60, 62

Adhesives: for tablestone repair, 74-75; in composite stone repair, 75; in slate repair, 83; in crypt repair, 86; mentioned, 72

Aerial photography, 36

Algae, 60

Anthropology, 21

Archaeology, 8, 21, 41

Architecture, significance of stones regarding, 16; firms dealing in preservation of, 57; conservator of, 58, 83; drawings of, 83; mentioned, 2

Armatures, used in stone repair, 75

Art, gravestones as, 1, 2, 6; gravestones as significant to, 16, 60, 66, 78; collectors of, 87; mentioned, 93

Artifacts, archaeological, 1; gravestones as, 57, 87-88; mentioned, 13, 86

Artisans, 57, 72, 83

Atmospheric pollution. *See* Pollution.

Attitudes toward death, 2

Biological growth, 27, 60, 63. *See also* Algea, Lichen, Fungus

Blistering, as stone deterioration, 27

Box tombs, 83, 84, 86

Brickwork, 48, 56, 83, 84

Bureaucratic considerations regarding graveyard care, 46

Cameras, choice of, 29, 35

Carbonaceous deposits, 60

Caretakers, and control of rubbing, 13; and documentation storage, 37; and yard maintenance, 47; and fragment care, 48; and museums, 88; mentioned, 87

Carvers: study of, 2, 19; examples of work, 6; signature of, 17, 28, 29, 36, 67; style

of, 24; identification of, 27, 29; mentioned, 88. *See also* Recarving stone

Casting, 69-71, 78. *See also* Replicas

Cataloguing, 51. *See also* Documentation

Cemeterians, 57

Cemetery, defined, 6; regulations for, 7, 13; management of, 13; mentioned, 68. *See also* Rural cemetery movement

Cleaning of stones, 25, 35, 58-59; agents for, 35

Clovers, 50, 54

Community support, 13, 16; mentioned, 59, 91

Collectibles, gravestones as, 87

Commerce, related to gravestones, 1

Composite stone, 74, 90

Condition report, 73

Conservation, defined, 6; of stone, 56; mentioned, 51, 52, 53, 56, 57, 71. *See also* Professionals

Conservator, 57, 58, 72. *See also* Professionals

Consultants, 56, 57, 83

Contractors, 56, 57, 58

Coping stones, 54

Craftsmen, 2, 67, 78

Crypts, 26, 72, 83, 86

Daughters of American Revolution, 21

Day of Judgment, 65

Descendants, 8, 20, 87

Deterioration, of stone, 6, 27, 48; and freeze-thaw cycle, 52, 66; and buried stones, 53; and sandblasting, 59; and cleaning stones, 62; of adhesive, 74; of sandstone, 78, 83; and need to remove stones from site, 86-87, 88; mentioned, 91. *See also* Acid rain, Pollution

Documentation, considering in establishing plan, 7; of archaeological work, 40;

and caretakers, 48; of fragments, 51, 53; and resetting, 65, 67, 71; of conservation work, 72-74; mentioned, 59, 83

Efflorescence, 27, 70, 71, 84
Epitaphs, and genealogy, 2;as information, 17, 20; reading of, 23; transcribing, 23, 24; documentation of, 59; and resetting stones, 67
Epoxies, 74
Erosion, 24, 27, 86
Exfoliation, 27, 83

Fences, 18
Fertilizers, 48, 54
Flaking, as stone deterioration, 27, 61
Foliage, 48, 55, 60
Folk art, 2, 21
Footstones, documention of, 26; used in carver attribution, 29; common positioning of, 65; uncovered by probing, 72; mentioned, 63
Fractures in stone, 61, 66
Fragments, recording of, 27; storage of, 51, 53; and freeze-thaw deterioration, 66; resetting of, 69-71; repair of, 75, 78; probing for, 71, 72; mentioned, 43, 48, 86, 91. See also Documentation
Funding, planning for, 8; for removal of stones, 91; mentioned, 36, 46, 51, 54, 56, 59, 60
Fungi, 60, 88

Garden clubs, 22
Genealogy, 2, 21
Geology, 20, 21
Graffiti, 27
Granite, 27, 66
Grants, 20, 21
Grant writing, 8
Grass cutters, nylon whip, 47, 50
Grave rails, 40
Graveyard preservation, 59, 86. See also Specific areas of preservation
Graveyard preservation consultant. See Professionals
Graveyard, defined, 6. See also Specific topics regarding graveyards

Groundcovers, 48, 50, 54
Guides, for graveyard visitors, 16; in photographing stones, 35; for stone restoration, 72

Headstone, documenting, 26; used in identifying fragments, 51; sunken, 63; common positioning of, 65; found by probing, 72
Herbicides, 48, 50
History, gravestones as, 1-3, 6; consideration of, in education, 16; gravestones of value to, 60, 66, 78; consideration of, in removing stones, 86, 87, 88. See also Professionals
Horticulture, 21
Horticulturist, 56
Humor of gravestones, 3

Iconography, 2
Inscriptions on stones, in education, 19; eroded, 86; mentioned, 3, 35, 60, 63, 65, 88
Instability of stone, 14, 61, 62, 66

Jurisdiction of graveyards. See Legal jurisdiction

Landscape architect, 55, 56
Landscaping, 8, 23
Legal considerations, and stone removal, 87, 88, 89; and graveyard legislation, 91; regarding jurisdiction, 7, 46
Lichens, 14, 24, 60
Lighting, 7, 18
Limestone, English, 1; and herbicides, 48; etched by biological growth, 60; cleaning of, 61, 62, 63; mentioned, 57

Maintenance of yards, problems of, 54; of grounds, 57; staff, 61, 65; mentioned, 8, 16, 18
Maps, 23
Marble, Carrara, 1; suggestions for rubbing, 14; documenting, 27; and herbicides, 48; and vines, 48; cleaning of, 60-63; resetting of, 66-67, 70; crypt repair, 86; mentioned, 57, 78, 86